A
Sincere
and
Constant
Love

An Introduction to the
Work of Margaret Fell

Edited with Introductions by T.H.S. Wallace

Friends
United Press
Richmond, Indiana • www.fum.org/shop

Copyright © 1992 by T.H.S. Wallace
Second Edition 2009

Published by Friends United Press,
101 Quaker Hill Dr., Richmond, Indiana 47374

Library of Congress Cataloging—In Publication Data

Fox, Margaret Askew Fell, 1614-1702.
A Sincere and Constant Love: An Introduction to the Work of Margaret Fell/ edited with introductions by T.H.S. Wallace.
p. cm.
Includes bibliographical references and index. 1. Society of Friends—Doctrines. 2. Fox, Margaret Askew Fell, BX7617.F885S5 1991
289.6'092-dc20   91-24187
CIP

CONTENTS

Preface..5
Preface to the Second Edition 13
Acknowledgments...19

Chapter 1: A True Testimony from the People of God....................21
Historical Introduction 21
Content Introduction...23
The Pamphlet 35
      Epistle to the Reader 36
      A True Testimony, Etc. 40

Chapter 2: A Declaration of Quaker Principles and Practice... 75
Historical Introduction 75
Content Introduction...78
The Declaration 82

Chapter 3: Women's Speaking Justified... 93
Historical Introduction 93
Content Introduction...95
The Pamphlet 99
      Women's Speaking Justified... 99
      A Further Addition... 113

Chapter 4: Some Ranters' Principles Answered........................121
Historical Introduction 121
Content Introduction...125
Some Ranters' Principles Answered 129

Chapter 5: Margaret Fell Fox in Her Own Words......................149
Historical and Content Introduction 149
    The Mystery Letter 149
    A Relation and A Testimony 153
    The Last Words 155
The Mystery Letter 157
A Relation of Margaret Fell... 160
The Testimony of Margaret Fell... 174
Some of the Sayings of Margaret Fox... 187

Study Guide...189

Appendices..209
George Whitehead's Testimony Concerning...Margaret Fell... 209
Domination, Submission, and the New Creation 211
A Note on Sources..216
Endnotes 217
Bibliography 228
Index..231

PREFACE

My chief aim in editing the handful of items from Margaret Fell's writings that comprise this volume is to make them, and thus, their author, more available to the modern reader.

It is long past time that Margaret Fell receives the notice due her. Her contemporaries in the early Quaker movement termed her its "nursing mother"—for her home in the 1650s became not only one of the centers of their spiritual network, but also one of their major administrative and communications focal points. Her decisions, material assistance, and spiritual support kept many Quaker ministers in the field in spite of the most adverse conditions and hostile opposition. By the 1660s, she became one of the clear leaders of the Society of Friends, lobbying with the Crown and Court for religious toleration and an end to the mass imprisonments of Quakers—a lobbying effort so difficult that at one juncture fifteen months of her sustained work in London were needed to effect its goals. Her ability to represent the Quaker movement was second only to that of its foremost preacher, George Fox. Her grasp of its principles and practices was unquestionably clear and sound.

The late Lewis Benson, one of the foremost scholars on the early Quaker movement and George Fox, characterized Margaret's grasp of the Quaker vision as capturing the very essence of the message of George Fox, a pristine distillation of all that was most important. In an unpublished letter on April 30, 1984, to Bonnelyn Young Kunze, a scholar laboring on a new biography of Margaret Fell, he characterized the latter's writing as coming

> ...closer to Fox's thought and teaching than the writing of any other early Friends'.... Although her writings are always in harmony with Fox they do not strike me as imitative or derived. She has made Fox's message her own message and, like Fox, she employs scripture language and scripture terms. But her writing comes through as a strong personal testimony.

More, Benson described Fell as a key figure in the founding generation of the Society of Friends:

> Unlike [William] Penn, [Robert] Barclay, and [Isaac] Penington, Margaret Fell was not an *apologist* for Quakerism. Like [Francis] Howgill and [Stephen] Crisp she belongs to the era of prophetic proclamation. Launching the early Quaker movement would have been difficult without her help.[1]

In the area of feminist studies, Fell's importance receives more recognition. She is cited as one of the first women to write espousing women's spiritual equality with men, and as a tireless promoter of the establishment of Women's Meetings, in which women were responsible for their own business affairs within the body of believers. By the nineteenth century, it was the Quaker Women's Meetings that supplied many women with the business and leadership experiences needed to become early leaders in a variety of social movements, from abolition through suffrage to feminism. Clearly, to neglect Margaret Fell's role and work in the growth of early Quakerism is essentially to neglect coming to a full understanding of the significance and impact of the Quaker movement and message on seventeenth century England and America—and beyond.

Yet, in spite of her importance, Margaret Fell has received negligible historical notice. Her own writings were gathered into a collection only once after her death.[2] The last hundred years of Quaker scholarship has produced only three biographies,[3] the latest and most thorough of which is Isabel Ross's, *Margaret Fell: Mother of Quakerism* in 1949.[4] Ross's volume, while historically astute, is unfortunately outdated and misleading in its discussion of the early Quaker apostolic vision and theology.

Regrettably, during the third quarter of the twentieth century, the interest of the Society of Friends in its spiritual and historical origins was minimal. Occasionally, one or another of Fell's pamphlets appeared, usually in facsimile, as movements with one social agenda, or another found her frank, vigorous observations related to their political concerns.

Fortunately, the last decade has seen a significant growth in popular and scholarly interest in the origins of early Quakerism. This has occurred in part due to a search by many within the Society of Friends for that faith and power that marked early Quakers, and in part to general historical interest in the seventeenth century English political scene spawned by the works of Christopher Hill and others.[5] Within the Society of Friends, Lewis Benson's pioneering work on George Fox's theology from 1942-1986 laid the foundation for further important work within the Society. Douglas Gwyn's major study, *Apocalypse of the Word: The Life and Message of George Fox,* is early fruit. In 1989, Joseph Pickvance's, *A Reader's Companion to the Journal of George Fox,* and T. Canby Jones' new edition of Fox's epistles, *The Power of the Lord is Over All,* both found ready audiences. Other works may soon appear. An edition of Fox's important, but heretofore unpublished, late sermons is being prepared by Max

Skinner of Canada. Arthur Windsor of England is completing his labor on a major index to George Fox's *Epistles*.

With this growing focus on Fox has come a concomitant increase in interest in other early Quaker figures, Margaret Fell included. Bonnelyn Young Kunze is preparing a forthcoming study, *Margaret Fell and the Rise of Quakerism*. And, of course, this present volume of Margaret Fell's work arises directly out of the increasing interest and ferment over the original Society of Friends.

Further study of Fell will also yield historical concerns, beyond those of the Quakers. Her concern for seventeenth century Jewish immigrants to England, and her writings directed to them, present an interesting and unusually sensitive chapter in the checkered history of the Jews and Britain. Her labors against anarchist elements threatening Quakerism are worth reading in relation to any study tracing the evolution of that political stance. Clearly, Fell's full and long life, extensive works, and vigorous witness, make her a figure to study.

My aim here is to increase the availability of her work in hopes of sparking further popular interest in, and serious scholarship on, her life, work, and message. To accomplish that aim, I have selected a representative sample from her extensive writings—a sample which contains those works of perhaps greatest immediate historical interest to both present day researchers and individuals seeking nourishment and direction in the early Quaker vision. Making them available, though, has not only meant bringing them physically back into print, but making them more easily available to the average reader for whom the syntax and style of seventeenth century English sometimes becomes a daunting adventure in grammatical contortion.

Even veteran researchers can find seventeenth century English style less than easily readable. Two of the key determinants of the readability of any text are: (1) difficult words (defined very roughly as words of three or more syllables) and (2) sentence length. While early Quaker writers rarely violated the rule of simple diction, they romped like most writers of their time through interminably long sentences. Margaret Fell is no exception.

Her stylistic practices are typical of those of seventeenth century English—the English of a language yet to undergo even the semistandardization brought to it by later grammarians and lexicographers. The run-on sentence is not only commonplace but a stock in trade. The repetitive use of the conjunction "and" as an easy and unnecessary transition abounds. It is not uncommon to have a sentence run-on through more than half a dozen sentence structures before the reader's tenuous and exhausted comprehension stumbles upon the oasis of a period. Liberal use of commas throughout the text, sometimes neither important to meaning nor reading, further fragments the reader's attention. Other punctuation, such as the semicolon, appears less often, but the rules governing usage were vague and observed in a desultory fashion. Such desultory usage is complicated further by the likelihood that most, if not all, of the works herein were dictated by Fell, in much the same fashion that George Fox dictated his *Journal*. Such dictation, reinforced by the preaching style of the day which was repetitive in content, may well account for much of the loose, redundant nature of Margaret Fell's style.

Considering that long grammatical constructions lead to difficulty in comprehension, I have eliminated the conjunction "and" and similar repetitive connectors (e.g., "but" or "for") wherever they appear to be superfluous and wherever their removal in no way alters the essential meaning and flow of the text. That is, I have simply broken Margaret Fell's ponderous multi-sentence constructions into their separate sentences. Where I have run upon ambiguity, or worse, unclearness, I have made no attempt to clarify the original. These practices have produced a somewhat more pleasing variety of sentences in the text and a greater sense of the strong rhetorical flow of Fell's writing. However, the reader will find many long convoluted sentences have resisted my reduction and remain as adventures.

Another seventeenth century rhetorical practice I have tried to refine (but only slightly) is the use of parallel structuring in sentences—that love of building one's thought through a torrent of similarly structured grammatical phrases. The device, refined to perfection by the modern speech writer, gave us the ringing phrases of Martin Luther King, Jr.'s, "I Have a Dream" speech, and John F. Kennedy's inaugural address. However, the device itself is as old as language and rhetoric and lent much power to Fell's preaching. In fact, its presence in Margaret Fell's work may have been reinforced through the act of dictation and suggests that reading the text aloud may increase both comprehension and effect. My refinements of Fell's parallelisms have largely been ones of addition—the addition of a word or two to a phrase obviously meant to be a segment of the larger rhetorical series, but missing the appropriate parallelism due to the vagaries of dictation, transcription, and printing. Additions to Margaret Fell's text are denoted by brackets. I worked diligently to keep their number low.

A third characteristic of seventeenth century style was the capitalization of most nouns, another vagary of unstandardized language. Religious practice since Fell's time has maintained capitalization in reference to doctrinal concepts ("The Light") and pronouns referring to the Godhead. However, as the reader will find, Fell's work is replete with religious argument, so full that adherence to any standard of capitalization, except the most simple, modern, and "secular" rules of grammar, becomes an editorial nightmare of surreal proportions. True to the Quaker testimony on simplicity, I have uncumbered the text of its inconsistent capitalization, except for a few instances,[6] discovering no meaning or intent lost in the process.

A special note is needed in relation to the many scriptural references with which Fell chose to undergird her text. The reader must be careful not to misinterpret and confuse her practice with that of modern Fundamentalist proof-texting. Her aim is not to create a collage of scripture verses ripped from context, but to present the *original* intent of the writer of the passage. Both Fell and Fox are remarkably modern in their understanding of scripture. They strive to consider the exact context within which each of the books of the Bible was produced (in so far as the context could be ascertained in their time). In fact, Fell's comprehensive and thorough understanding of the Bible enabled her to write a stunning refutation (see *Women's Speaking*) of those who selectively used Paul's comments in his epistles to deny women the right to participate in ministry—a refutation as timely in our century as in hers. Fell and Fox were not alone in their understanding of scripture. Most of the early Quaker leadership had the same breadth of knowledge and depth of vision, well tried because it was constantly called on to expose those who twisted texts, ignored contexts, and mutilated scripture for the most dubious purposes. The early Quakers could be devastating in their rebuttals, as Fell was in her scathing *An Answer to Ranters' Principles*, a refutation that reveals just how badly Quaker opponents could bastardize the scriptures for their purposes.

In her scripture references, Fell usually uses a short verse citation, the verse itself being intimately related to her purposes. Yet, when one checks the context, it too is intimately relevant to the points being made and enlarges our understanding of the Quaker interpretation and vision of scripture. Thus, I have cited, on many occasions, the larger context to which her reference points.

One might, after reading this analysis of Margaret Fell's style, be tempted to consign her to the ranks of the unlettered. Such a response would be more than a gross injustice; it would frankly reveal intellectual blindness. It would deny the historical and lingual contexts in which she lived. The quality of Fell's prose in her day was more than merely acceptable; it was good enough to be received by the chief executive and leading men of her nation. Her papers and declarations were received and read by the intellectual elite of her time—and taken seriously. Care was taken either to respond to them or rebut them depending on the reader's position. According to the vague language standards of the time, Fell's prose was quite acceptable—in fact, on a par with educated usage. A quick comparison of Fell's work with Samuel Pepys' famous *Diary* and John Bunyan's *The Pilgrim's Progress* will quickly demonstrate that she was a respectable stylist in her time.

In fact, the sensitive reader will come to enjoy the quickness of Fell's mind, the clearness of her vision, her fundamental grasp of law and theology, her stunning understanding of scripture, her ability to cut cleanly through the obfuscations of opponents, be they priests or the King's Justices, to the heart and soul of what was at stake in the argument. To misread her would be to miss an enlivening contact with an indomitable woman as tough-minded as any of the men of her age. To dismiss her would be to dismiss one of the key female founders of early Quakerism, a woman much of its membership considered, in the words of John Stubbs, a most "dear counsellor and comforter."

T.H.S. Wallace
Camp Hill, Pennsylvania
January 1992

PREFACE TO THE SECOND EDITION

When I began my study in the early 1980s of Margaret Fell and her ministry, I saw that study as a path to better understanding the early Quaker vision, faith, and practice. After all, in Fell we have one of the early converts of George Fox—a woman who more clearly understood Fox's dynamic experience and understanding of the original Christian gospel than anyone else. It was Fell who quickly turned her home into a key communication and support node for the growing Quaker movement. It was she who fostered a Quaker community on her estate at Swarthmore Hall. And it was she who, twenty years after her convincement and fifteen years after her widowhood, became Fox's helpmate in marriage and co-partner in ministry. Fell's experience, work, and ministry, when paired with Fox's, became one of the most important pillars supporting the growth and development of Quaker faith and practice.

My work on Fell took some ten years and proved a work of faith. Lewis Benson, the foremost George Fox scholar of his day and the man who helped direct my early research on Fell, once asked, "If and when you finish this work, what are you going to do with it?" A key question to which my only answer was, "I work in hope that it will find a publisher, when it is ready." That faith was confirmed in 1992 when Friends United Press (FUP) chose to publish *A Sincere and Constant Love*. I'm further grateful to FUP for keeping the volume in print over the ensuing seventeen years, and recognizing the need for a new edition.

That need rests on several facts. When the first edition appeared, it was critically well received, but did not receive the wide notice for which both FUP and I had hoped. FUP, like many small presses in the 1980s and 1990s, had not yet begun using ISBNs (International Standard Book Numbers). Lacking an ISBN meant that the work would not be listed in *Books in Print* and other key publishing reference volumes, and thus it did not come to the attention of a larger reading public. Regrettably, the volume went generally unnoticed by non-Quaker readers and scholars, and even some recent Quaker scholarship has been unaware of the work. Thus, I was delighted when Trish Edwards-Konic, former FUP editor, and then Katie Terrell, present editor, explored the possibility of a new edition with me.

The Significance of A Sincere and Constant Love

When Margaret Fell heard George Fox preach in Ulverston steeple house in 1652, she cried bitterly, "We are all thieves; we are all thieves. We have taken the scriptures in words, and know nothing of them in ourselves." She was experiencing a profound realization, an understanding that many in our own day still miss: that true faith in Christ Jesus is founded on the experience of His powerful resurrected living presence and His ability to lead, teach, and direct us in our faith.

A Sincere and Constant Love remains the only study to describe, accurately and in detail, Fell's faith, practice, and experience in terms of the everlasting gospel revealed to George Fox. It is the first work to avoid the all too common scholarly error of interpreting early Quaker faith through the lens of the Quakerism scholars found prevalent in their own times. It also avoids the error of recent studies which grossly inflate secular influences on early Friends, while de-emphasizing the powerful—yea, the overriding—influence of spiritual experience and spiritual leading. While these works proudly trumpet that they do not commit the error of parochialism, they simply ignore their own secular and academic biases, while claiming "historiographic objectivity."

Fell and the many women ministers who traveled hundreds, even thousands, of miles to preach the gospel have received nowhere near the credit and study they deserve. They were followers, not of male leaders but of their One Guide and Leader, Jesus Christ. In following Him and His direction, they became leaders in their own right, spiritual equals with their male counterparts, and spiritual equals who often carried the gospel message to new cities and countries ahead of those counterparts. Like the latter, those women suffered beatings, imprisonments, loss of goods, and even loss of life as they followed their Lord.

Margaret Fell's Writings: A Continuing Relevance

As I reviewed once again Fell's pamphlets printed here, they struck me as even more relevant to us now. For instance, in a time when too many believe they can have "gospel order" without the gospel, a Christ Jesus but not to rule over them, an edifice of social justice without a spiritual foundation, or that they can empower people while ignoring the power of God, Margaret Fell's *A True Testimony of the People of God...* points us to the one sure foundation for faith and action in our world.

In a time when much is made of particular Quaker testimonies—such as the peace testimony—as more important than others, Fell reminds us that all testimonies are meant to serve as a unified witness to the presence and power of Christ Jesus leading and teaching us. Fell's *A Declaration and Information from us, The People Called Quakers*—which predates its more famous progeny, the 1661 *Declaration from the Harmless and Innocent People of God called Quakers*,

Against All Plotters and Fighters in the World (better known today as the Quaker Peace Testimony), and served as its blueprint—is instructive today of the spiritual and scriptural origins of the Quaker witness that all are equal before God's eyes and is grounds for some of the seemingly more peculiar manifestations to that witness. While some readers today may feel that such testimonies as the use of thee and thou, the avoidance of titles, and the refusal to make elaborate obeisance to those of higher social standing were arcane and esoteric, Fell recognized failure to make one's witness in small things substantially weakens one's ability to take a major stand when it is required.

Given that the early Quaker faith and revelation was the first since early Christian times to produce an apostolic ministry of men and women spiritually laboring together as equals, far more notice needs to be focused on Fell's pamphlet, *Women's Speaking Justified*.... That pamphlet remains one of the best explanations of the scriptural basis for women's spiritual equality and women's full participation in the spiritual labors of the church. Even today we find women's ministry restricted, rejected, and silenced not only in many Protestant evangelical pastoral ministries, but also in the Roman Catholic and Orthodox priesthoods. Even in those denominations in which women have received ordination and some recognition, their work is still often quietly neglected or denigrated by fellow male clergy. The solid scriptural arguments that Fell levels at those who keep spirit-led women silent should long since have begun to resolve the debate on this issue. It is largely ignorance of her work and George Fox's that allow such spiritual stifling to continue.

The thinking Fell addresses in her small pamphlet, *Some Ranters' Principles Answered*, is thinking that has become endemic to, and epidemic among, Western European and American cultural elite. Relativism, Deconstructionism, Post-modernism, and their philosophical cousins are simply updated mutations of Ranterism—mutations made fashionable for a supposed New Age. Fell's blunt and angry demolition of the Ranter vision is a fitting first dose of a much needed anecdote to a philosophical poison that today goes largely unchallenged and sickens our time, our spiritual lives, and the general body politic.

If there is for today's reader an "off-putting" element in Margaret Fell's writing, it is not in her ideas, but in her tone. To our ears, Fell's combative tone sounds fierce, denunciatory, condemnatory—intolerant. However, her intolerance is an intolerance of injustice, deceit, lies, irrationality, exploitation, and persecution. Fell is the stalwart voice of Truth and, as her opponents—including the judges at her trials—learned, Truth will not be silenced.

My recommended antidote to those offended by her tone? Hear once again the strong, firm voice of Truth which brooks no falsehood, no trickery, slick sleight of tongue, and demands only simple, clear, and healthy honesty. Hear the babble of Babylon for what it is. Begin to know the freedom of the Word and speak clearly with forthrightness untypical in our day. Begin to speak with the clarity, freedom, and force of Margaret Fell.

Finally, I am thankful that FUP has decided to add a Study Guide to *A Sincere and Constant Love*. In designing the guide, I utilized an ancient Quaker approach: as our first Friends measured their lives and faith by the lives and faith of the first Christians, so the accompanying Study Guide aims to help today's Friends and seekers after Truth to measure their lives, faith, and witness against those of our earliest and most faithful Friends. It aims to help us answer that most central early Quaker question: Do we live in the love and power, and speak with the authority which we see in Christ Jesus, the prophets, and the apostles?

T.H.S. Wallace
Camp Hill, Pennsylvania
May 28, 2009

ACKNOWLEDGMENTS

I am grateful for the encouragement, advice, and help of many people in compiling this volume. Assistance came from both sides of the Atlantic. Joseph Pickvance of Birmingham, England, was especially helpful in the securing of texts. The late Lewis Benson strongly encouraged me in my studies of early Quakerism and made many useful suggestions on which of Margaret Fell's many works deserve to be brought forward first. Milton Ream, formerly of the Haverford College Quaker Collection, was instrumental in securing the text of Margaret Fell's, *A Brief Collection of Remarkable Passages*…, without which my work could not have progressed. Patricia Edwards, whose ongoing interest and study of Margaret Fell parallels my own, has been encouraging throughout the project.

The patience and faith of my wife, Diane, was notably helpful and has seen me through the joys and vicissitudes of word processing. Lucy Talley of Evanston, Illinois, rendered especially insightful advice that brought the manuscript into its final form. Response from early readers of the typescript—in the United States, Great Britain, and Kenya—was especially encouraging, and, finally, the interest and assistance of Douglas Gwyn and Patricia Edwards proved particularly helpful in placing the manuscript. From the beginning, this edition of Margaret Fell's work was an act of faith—faith that the labor could be brought to fruit, faith that she would again find appreciative readers, and faith that her works would again see print and inspire new generations of readers. Such work is actually the labor of many hands and minds, and for their assistance, I am grateful.

CHAPTER 1

A TRUE TESTIMONY
FROM THE PEOPLE OF GOD
(WHO BY THE WORLD
ARE CALLED QUAKERS)

Historical Introduction

A *True Testimony* is one of Margaret Fell's key doctrinal pamphlets. It is an excellent introduction to the message proclaimed by seventeenth century Quakers and how that gospel was markedly different from the message other Christian bodies were declaring. A *True Testimony* also provides a good entry into the scriptural basis of Quaker thinking, for while Friends directed people "to the Spirit that gave forth the scriptures, by which they might be led into all truth," they also claimed their faith was thoroughly grounded in scripture. As George Fox observed, looking back on his own experiences:

> ...I had no slight esteem of the Holy Scriptures, but they were very precious to me, for I was in that spirit by which they were given forth, and what the Lord opened to me I afterwards found was agreeable to them. (*Journal*, Nickalls edition, 34)

This agreeableness with scripture was of utmost importance, not only for Fox, but for Quakers in general. They viewed scripture as an essential source book of spiritual experience. The workings and fruits of the spirit in the lives of the prophets, Jesus Christ, and his apostles served as a measuring rod and a check for first Friends. Spiritual experiences and revelations that contradicted the doctrines and testimony of scripture were to be immediately suspect. When Margaret Fell claims, on the title page of *A True Testimony*, that the doctrines and witness of Friends are identical in both power and spirit with those of the prophets, Christ, and his apostles, she asserts the truth of Quaker experience, and with it the radical consequences and profound import of the Gospels for her time and for ours.

The composition date of *A True Testimony* has not been established. However, its composition probably preceded by only a few months its printing in 1660. Normally, there was little delay in printing because of Quaker passion to get the word out and to clarify positions. This, of course, was of exceptional importance in 1660 with the final collapse of the Puritan Revolution and the return of the monarchy in May of 1660. Quakers viewed the restoration with both concern and hope: *concern* that persecution by Puritans might merely be replaced by a repressive Crown seeking vengeance on religious nonconformists; *hope* that Quaker lobbying could make clear to the Crown that Friends were a harmless people who sought the good of all, *hope* that the Crown would seek the broad road with an Act of Religious Toleration. It was a lobbying effort that Margaret Fell was to be involved in, not only through her pamphlets, but also as a major representative of Friends before the Crown and Court. *A True Testimony* was likely a part of the "information of our principles" that Margaret Fell reports[1] presenting to the King at Whitehall in 1660.

Content Introduction

A True Testimony is prefaced by an "Epistle to the Reader," prophetic and urgent in tone. The language of the epistle's first page is rooted in the Revelation of John. However, one must be careful not to confuse the Quaker understanding of John's Revelation with millennialist or modern Fundamentalist thinking. The difference is momentous.

Douglas Gwyn has pointed out, in *The Apocalypse of the Word*, that early Friends, Margaret Fell, and George Fox:

> understood the problem of the Church in terms of the Book of Revelation and its portrayal of a demonic religious and political force in conflict with the rule of Christ. This power is seen to be at war with the true Church, attempting to break the obedience of the faithful through coercion and seduction. (212)

This power, the Beast, its Babylon, and false prophets of the book of Revelation, had manifested itself in the institutional church and its schisms into various denominations. These institutions took their authority from something other than God, from the authority of men who rely on religious and state hierarchies to maintain their power or from the Bible as the word of God, (instead of Jesus Christ, the Word). Since these groups rejected the authority of Jesus, his manifestation, leading, and direction in the human heart, early Friends claimed that Christendom had fallen into darkness and away from the Gospel of Christ over the 1,600 years of its history. However, with the revelation and manifestations of the power of God in Friends' lives, preaching, and work, God was reasserting Himself in history. The long centuries of confusion and apostasy from the apostolic experience of the risen Christ were seen coming to an end.

Early Friends believed that, as the prophetic and apostolic Church restored, they incarnated Christ's life-and-death battle against Satan as envisioned in Revelation. Christ had come to teach his people himself, fulfilling the vision of Revelation 19 of the divine warrior come down from heaven to war against the false religion. This cosmic conflict, which Friends called "The Lamb's War," was not a battle waged with carnal weapons, but a spiritual warfare carried forth in the preaching and adamant nonconformity of Friends under first Puritan and then Anglican persecutions. (Gwyn, 212)

Thus, when Fell declares in *A True Testimony*, "the day of the Lord is come," she is announcing Christ Jesus come again to do battle with all spiritual force.

But what of the utter end of history? The final triumph and judgment? The Second Coming as envisioned by ranks upon ranks of millennialists and Fundamentalists over time? Fox and other Friends, Gwyn notes,

made no bold predictions about the time or manner of the final outcome, but it was his repeated assertion that "the Lamb shall have the victory." (212)

That claim remains true to the essential vision and message of the Revelation of John.

From the urgency of her interpretation of Revelation, Fell moves to state the essence of the gospel and of her *Testimony*. Essentially, the light of Christ shines in people's hearts—"where God's appearance and manifestation is, where He writes His law," and where He empowers people to obey his will through the presence of His spirit.

Her assertion that the light is both for Jews and Gentiles, and that, by it, the Gentiles "can do the things contained in the law," is one of particular importance. Traditional Christian thinking doomed those who lived before Christ's earthly appearance, and those who never heard of Him, at best to purgatory, at worst to damnation. However, Quakers saw the ridiculousness of this position, proclaiming that Jesus Christ is unchangeable, the same yesterday, today, and tomorrow, and by His unlimited power He could manifest His spirit in men and women to do right and reject wrong in any age. Quaker doctrine is truly universal and timeless and certainly in line with Paul's justification of the Gentiles in Romans (which Fell will stress later in her *Testimony*). Opposed to this universalism stands "the worship…set up in the nations" by men in "their own inventions, imaginations, meanings, and expositions of the scriptures without them, men who draw people away from the light and spirit of God within them." Thus, Fell urges her readers to read *A True Testimony* seriously, weigh her words in their conscience, and search and check what she says against scripture and the spirit. These three should be sufficient to confirm the truth in what she is saying.

Fell begins the body of her argument by restressing its universality—"to all the professed teachers in the whole world, who go under the name of Christians"—and moves rapidly to establish the existence of the apostasy, the failure of Christendom over the last 1,600 years to follow Christ. The testimony such Christians have borne "is only the letter of the scriptures." Fell is rather exact in identifying the appearance of the apostasy after the Gospels, Acts, and the Epistles were written during the period when the Revelation of John was composed. As she observes: "the antichristian spirit entered in amongst them, for the apostle John saw in his time that the antichrist was come."

The original Quaker claim of the apostasy was as difficult for seventeenth century Christians to accept as it is for those of the twenty-first century and thus needs clarification. First, the word "apostasy" itself is instructive. It means "to fall away" or "to stand aside" from one's faith. For original Friends and early Christians, the direct revelation by Christ of Himself to His followers and within their hearts began to be supplanted by man-directed and mediated religion, by "Christians" who no longer relied directly on their present Lord for direction and for power to do His will. Thus, they no longer trusted, nor had faith in His power.

Second, in recognizing the presence of the apostasy, early Quakers were *not* claiming that it was complete, that God manifested Himself to no peoples during the long period of Christian history. Such a claim would have been to deny the power of God to reach men and women in any age, and the first Quakers were never ones to question that power. However, the history of the institutional churches, whether Catholic or Protestant, had been one of relying on the authority of a church hierarchy or of the scriptures, rather than on the authority of the spirit and its leading.

Third, Margaret Fell, true to her opening statement in this pamphlet, claims a scriptural basis for the apostasy. She carefully assembles the prophetic evidence that Christ, Paul, and Peter all predicted the appearance of antichrists and false prophets.

Fourth and finally, Fell turns to the physical evidence of the apostasy in her own time, the multitude of religions and sects that appeared since the apostles' days and that demonstrate by their violent behavior and disunity that they do not walk in unity with the Prince of Peace.

For Fell, a sign of how utterly thorough the apostasy had become lies in the fact that in her own day, when the Truth was manifested in Friends' preaching, it was denounced as the work of false prophets. Her plain characterization of Christendom, however, is as true today as it was in her own time:

They, having their words and writings upon record, do make these a sufficient testimony for them of their knowledge and worship of God, and so preach, teach, take texts out of these words, add thereunto their own inventions, and so feed poor ignorant people with these.

Certainly, the confession of theologian W. Paul Jones in his 1981, *The Province Beyond the River*…, only seems to reinforce Fell's truth as relevant to our own times:

I am a theologian—I spend my life reading, teaching, thinking, writing, about God. I am mind, and I am action, attempting some sort of faithful mix of the two. But I must be honest—*I have never experienced God*, not really. I am embarrassed by piety; I am ill at ease with those who thrive on God talk; I have no awareness of what one might mean by the "presence of God." What would one conclude about a person spending her whole life dissecting, analyzing, and advocating love, but who has never herself been in love? Yet of many of my colleagues as with many of my students, I suspect what I suspect about myself—I am a professing Christian and a *functional atheist*. (3-4)

Fell succinctly characterizes what is at stake and what the chief difference is between Christendom and the Quakers:

Let the people seriously consider what they venture their souls upon, for it is not a deceitful lying spirit that will feed the soul. It is the spirit of life and truth that nourishes the soul and leads into all truth. Here is the chief difference between them and us: they have the words and declaration of Christ and the apostles, declared from the spirit of life; we have the spirit which these words were declared from. Not another, but the same eternal spirit which they had, do we witness and bear our testimony of: the same Christ (and not of another) which witnessed a good confession before Pontius Pilate and was crucified upon the cross of Jerusalem. This Christ, which all the Christians in Christiandom profess in words, do we bear testimony of in the spirit of life and power, according to the scriptures.

Having established her initial argument, Fell recognizes the anticipated objection. How have members of "an 'upstart religion' come to this spirit after such centuries of darkness?" In other words, what makes Quakers so special? In response, Fell claims nothing special for Friends. First, she asserts the objection is really "against the unlimited spirit and power of the living God." At this point, however, she raises a hard corollary for moderns: the possibility that God hardened hearts during the apostasy as He is said to have hardened Pharaoh's during Moses' time. In short, "the spirit of the Lord cannot be limited, but limits all according to the good pleasure of His will, that He may make his power known." Second, the truth of the apostasy and the Gospel were not received from men, "but by the immediate power and revelation of Jesus Christ, according to the work and operation of it in us." For those who balk at the idea of immediate revelation, Fell carefully points out key references in the epistles of Paul to establish it as the all important center of Christian doctrine and experience. Finally, Fell turns the tables on those by raising objections, suggesting that "the reason wherefore this spirit and revelation have been hid so many years" is "because people have erred from the spirit of God in them, through which the revelation is manifested."

Moving from her argument concerning the presence of apostasy, Fell opens the second key point of Quaker doctrine: What is true worship? The answer is direct, simple, and essential: that God is spirit and they that worship Him do so in spirit and in truth. They are the only true worshipers of God. She opens with a forceful series of queries worthy of a first class lawyer:

> I do ask all the teachers and professors in Christendom, where this spirit is that God is to be worshiped in, if it be not in man? How it is or can be attained to, any otherwise than by the light of Christ Jesus, with which He has lighted every man that comes into the world, in whom is life and this life is the light of men? Where this worship of God in the spirit is performed, if it be not in man? . . . How and where must people come to worship God in the spirit, which denies the light of Christ to be their leader and teacher, and say it is natural?

Fell reminds her readers that the Jews, who searched scripture and relied on its authority alone, failed to recognize the anointed Son of God when He appeared. She draws the sharp parallel between them and the professed Christians and churchmen of her own day, ironically observing "this may be the condition of the priests of the world and teachers of the letter." Her careful review of Johannine and Pauline scriptures, including Paul's crucial arguments concerning the inward and outward Jew (Romans 2), his introduction of the faith to the Athenians (Acts 17), and his descriptions of the body as the temple of God, stoutly reinforce her arguments from scripture.

Fell, then, moves to crucial observations in the epistles of Peter, especially Peter's directing those to whom he wrote to "the prophetic word made more sure." Fell's references to prophecy, to Jesus being "the spirit of prophecy," need illumination in our time, a time that sees prophecy as merely predicting the future. However, in scripture, among early Christians, and among first Friends, the foretelling role of the prophets was not chief among their purposes and only grew out of their far more important work of calling the people out of wrong doing into obedience to God's will and bringing them a word or message directly from God. In these latter roles, Jesus serves as "the spirit of prophecy," because He speaks directly to those who will listen, obey, and receive his power. He is the one who directly reveals the meaning of scripture and gives His messages to those who will hear.

Again, Fell is quick to anticipate objection to the doctrine of immediate revelation, stressing it is not new, "though it may seem so to many." She lays the reasons for this blindness on the "teachers of people" whose doctrine refuses to admit or sanction present day "revelation or inspiration by the spirit of God." They stop the free flow of spiritual water from Christ, the fountain whose spirit is unlimited and for all. Here, then, is another major difference between ministers of the world and "ministers of God and of the spirit." The latter "joy and desire that people grow in the light" where the faithful are brought to unity in the body of Christ and given the power to break the back of evil in their lives.

In fact, Margaret Fell, like George Fox and others of the Quaker apostolate, go so far as to assert that Christ's new and potent revelation of Himself among Quakers is part of the revelation that John foresaw and foretold in the last book of the Bible. As has already been noted, the original Quaker understanding of the Revelation of John is markedly different from modern Fundamentalist eschatology. For early Friends, the Revelation described God's triumphant revealing of Himself to His people. The second coming, Fell views in large part as being Christ's coming "the second time without sin unto salvation" to "all those that believe in Him, trust in Him, obey Him, and wait for Him." More, the gathering of God's people into spiritual unity is well captured in the image of the New Jerusalem, that city that needs no light because "God is its light, and its lamp is the Lamb" (Rev. 21:23f). As John's Revelation foresaw the triumph of Christ, so Margaret Fell energetically and confidently declares, "…it is vain to stand against the God of Heaven or resist His work which He…will work by His spirit in this His day of power."

Fell devotes the final fifteen pages of her pamphlet to exploring more closely what consequences develop from the worship of God in spirit and in truth. These consequences, she notes, cannot be learned from "the priests, teachers, and professors of the world," because they have no knowledge of the power of God to destroy sin (yea, they "teach all people to be sinners") and "know little of the pourings forth of the spirit." Margaret Fell declares, "Therefore, it's good for everyone to have a true testimony of this eternal spirit, which believes not every spirit, but tries them, whether they be of God, and proves all things, and holds fast that which is good."

The first great consequence of living life at the direction of Jesus is a coming into the fellowship of the Gospel, being founded on a sure foundation. When all look humbly to Christ for leadership, they are brought into a marked unity of spirit so that "if they were ten thousand they are all one." Even more important, this unity created by the power of God enables the faithful to weather the storms of life and persecution. However, Fell's emphasis here is on the faithful church weathering the tempest together, not as individuals weathering things alone, but for God. For Fell, "the unity in the spirit, which is the bond of peace," with others in the faith is a central necessity. God seeks a people to call His own, to lead and to be His witnesses to the world. The individual relationship with Christ Jesus is a *non sequitur* ("it does not follow"), if it is apart from the gathered people of God. Margaret is utterly frank on this point: those that deny the gathering power of the spirit cannot possibly be part of Christ's body. They are prostituting themselves and still pursuing something other than God.

The second great consequence of worshiping God in spirit and truth is that one experiences "the ministrations of the spirit." Those women and men who are moved by Christ Jesus to declare the Good News, to bring a message from the Lord, "reach into that of God in the hearts of people." "That of God" for early Quakers was *not a spark of divinity* in humankind, but a longing, a thirst for God, that only God could answer and fulfill. "That of God" recognizes the anointing of the spirit and therefore one is enabled by it to respond. With the coming of the spirit, Margaret declares, "such need not that any man should teach them, but as the same anointing teaches them…"—the essence of the new covenant described by both Jeremiah (31:31) and the Gospel and Letters of John. Not only does the spirit teach, it brings the daughters and sons of God liberty by inwardly working and operating to produce a meek and quiet spirit. It subdues fleshly desires—which for early Friends meant all those desires within (covetousness, pride, envy, wrath, etc.) that lead us away from God and following His will, that lead to lawless behavior—thus fostering a new person who, by inward direction, needed no outward rule of law. While Fell recognizes this may sound like foolishness to her opponents, she reminds them both of the significance of the Christ-the-cornerstone metaphor used extensively in the Old and New Testaments and of Paul's classic observation that the wisdom of God seems foolishness to men. Her interpretation alone of the metaphor is a classic piece of Quaker exegesis.

Further consequences flow when people come to, and walk by, Christ's eternal spirit. "All that do endeavor to keep the unity in the spirit and body of peace are strengthened by this spirit" in the inner person. People's understanding is enlightened and they come to comprehend the full love of God. They are "renewed in the spirit of their minds," their consciences are cleansed, and they bring forth "fruits of the spirit." They come out of transgression, new women and men producing the fruits of love, peace, gentleness, fairness, temperateness, etc. (See Gal. 5:22.) These fruits are important, for they are the signs of salvation and evidence of the presence of Christ.

In fact, the question of fruits is a key concern of Margaret Fell's pamphlet for she astutely and rightly observes Jesus' own emphasis on fruits. He identified them as the marks by which to try right and false spirits. Thus, Fell calls her readers to judge between the professing Christian and the Quaker: which one evidences the fruits of the flesh from adultery through murder, to witchcraft and wrath? However, as she reviews the scriptural lists of evil fruits, they become so long and dire she, herself, feels it necessary to address the objection she's fallen into harsh censoriousness. Indeed, many ministers, priests, and professing Christians seem to seek actively to evade the worst of these sins. Yet, she rightly observes that since they doctrinally declare that it is impossible to break the power of sin in this life, they in effect "stand in that ground which brings forth the fruits of the flesh," and thus, as teachers, are also guilty of the fruits of others who accept their teaching and thus fall into all manner of destructive behavior. As teachers, they fertilize the ground from which such evil grows. Thus, those who desire godliness and truth must turn from those who deny the power of God to those who seek it.

As a militant and prophetic voice of the early Quaker ministry, Margaret Fell is rarely more forceful than in her summary remarks in the *Testimony*. Her language is bold and tough—Christ's reign is coming. Her tense is present, is immediate. She calls people to hear His voice, the proclamation that now the law and testimony, long sealed among the disciples, is opened, and that the Word—Christ— is revealed: these are revolutionary claims of a new age, the final age when women and men will live by God's revelation in their hearts. This great mystery, "the mystery of godliness, God manifest in the flesh," is Margaret Fell's challenge, her call to a whole new way of worship and life. The essence of her Good News, the original Christian and Quaker Good News, radical and challenging in her own day, sounds to us even more so. Our own faith in the gods of science and psychology, technology and history, lead us to profess control of our lives and world, but the darkening frontiers and tragic failure of our century point to an opposite conclusion. To open ourselves to God's direction and control, to immediate revelation, and to empowerment by God, is a revolutionary challenge—a vision that can turn the present age upside down.

The Pamphlet

A True Testimony from the People of God
(Who by the World are Called Quakers)
of

The doctrines of the prophets, Christ, and the apostles, which are witnessed unto by them who are now raised up by the same power and quickened by the same spirit (and blood of the everlasting covenant) which brought again our Lord Jesus from the dead.

Published for this end, (viz.)

That all sober minded people may see the unity and agreement of our doctrine and testimony with the testimony of Jesus and all the holy men of God.

With the difference between us and them that have the form of words, but not the power thereof.

"Do not quench the Spirit, do not despise prophesying, but test everything; hold fast what is good, abstain from every form of evil" (1 Thess. 5:19-22).

"Now we have received not the spirit of the world, but the Spirit which is from God, for the Spirit searches everything, even the depths of God" ([hybrid of] 1 Cor. 2:12, 10).

First Printed in the Year 1660

Epistle to the Reader

Friend,

Being that the day of the Lord is come and He is arisen in His eternal light and is arising in the consciences of men, the place where His throne and scepter must rule the nations; being that He is king, lord, and lawgiver to those who are under His government and is the supreme head and judge in the consciences: now this being arisen and manifested in this day of the Lord's power, in which He will make all His people willing and subject to Him; being that this has been long obscured and covered with the thick veil of darkness and cloud of apostasy that have been over the face of the earth and indeed over the hearts of men; [being that] the only cause and reason of this has been the cup of abomination and fornication the nations have drunk in, the worship of the beast, upon which the whore sits, which John saw (when he stood upon the sand of the sea) rise up out of the sea, which all the world wondered after, insomuch that mystery Babylon the Great made all nations drunk with the cup of her fornication: Now the day is come that Babylon is come up in remembrance with the Lord.[1] The day of her judgments is come. The vials are pouring upon the seat and head of the beast. The darkness is expelling.

The light is arising out of obscurity and shining secretly in the hearts of people where God's appearance and manifestation are, where He writes His law, and puts His spirit in the inward parts—which is the new covenant which He has made with the house of Israel and with the house of Judah, and which is also a light to the Gentiles by which they can do the things contained in the law, having the substance of the law, which is light, written in their hearts. Their consciences [will] also bear them witness of the justice and righteousness of the law, when God comes to judge the secrets of their hearts by Jesus Christ, who is the end of the law for righteousness and who is the light that is given to be the salvation to the ends of the earth.

Now all people that come to be guided by this law, which is light—they by so doing come into God's covenant and promise. Coming into this light, covenant, and spirit which God puts in the inward parts, here all people meet together, Jews and Gentiles, barbarian, Scythian, bond and free, in the unity of the spirit which is in Christ Jesus our Lord, in which they come to be all one in Christ. If they be Christ's, then are they Abraham's seed and heirs, according to the promise (Gal. 3:29).

This is the great mystery that has been hid from ages and generations past, by reason of the gross darkness that has covered men. The great cause and reason of all this has been because the worship that has been set up in the nations has had its foundation in the darkness. The very root and ground of it has been darkness itself. The teachers and ministers thereof have been ministers of darkness and have not turned people from the darkness to the light, but on the contrary have drawn them from the light and spirit of God within them, unto their inventions, imaginations, meanings, and expositions of the scriptures without them. So [they] have been building Babel in the many languages which God is coming to confound. It may be they have read a chapter, then turn, pervert it, and mix with it their own dark imaginations of their evil hearts. Again, [they] read a verse of a chapter and make an hour's discourse of what they had intended and hatched up in their minds (it may be) a week before. Thus, they have fed poor people with chaff and husks, but the Lord is arisen in His mighty power, with His fan in His hand. He is separating the chaff from the wheat, is gathering the wheat into His garner, and will burn up the chaff with unquenchable fire.

Now, reader, in soberness and singleness of your heart, read this following treatise without an evil eye and a prejudiced mind. Let the truth of God have place in the heart. Let the light of Christ in your conscience seriously judge, weight the things therein contained, (according to the scriptures) prove all things, and holdfast that which is good. Look not at men, nor at the times, as they stand in relation to men, for in so doing, the god of the world will blind the eye. Look at the Lord, at His truth, and eye His dealing and dispensation of His will, according to His wisdom. Let Him be your fear. Let Him be your dread. Slight not your day of visitation of His love, for truly the Lord, whom we seek, will suddenly come to His temple, and who may abide the day of His coming, who will sift as a refiner's fire and will be as fuller's soap? Certainly He will plead with all flesh by sword and by fire and bring into the valley of Jehoshaphat.[2] All flesh will be as grass, the glory thereof as the flower of the field, when the spirit of the Lord blows upon it, because all people are grass. It is not flesh and blood that can enter into the kingdom of God, which He is now restoring unto Israel. It is that that will pass the fire of His jealousy and come through clear and pure, that will be accepted of in this His day. People have long made Him serve with their sins and wearied Him with their iniquities. Their worships and services have been an abomination unto Him. The fear that has been taught towards Him has been by the precepts of men. Flesh and blood have performed the worship that should have been to Him. Therefore has there been no entrance into the kingdom of God, but all have been kept back and out of the holy city. Though the gates have stood open by day, yet no unclean could enter, nor nothing that wrought abomination, or made a lie—for that is in the night of darkness and is out of the day, where the gates of the holy city stand open.

So now, reader, these things being set before you, in love unto you and to all people: slight them not, nor look lightly over them, for if you do seriously consider and weigh them with that of God in your conscience, you will find them truth and according to the scriptures of truth. Therefore, search and examine the following treatise by the scriptures and the spirit of truth. You will find that in your own bosom which will answer to the truth of what is here written. To the Lord I commit you, and to His witness in you, which will answer for His truth.

Margaret Fell

A True Testimony, Etc.

> To all the professed teachers in the whole world,
> who go under the name of Christians and make a
> profession of Christ (who was offered up at Jeru-
> salem, which the scriptures declare of), whether
> they are Jesuits, bishops, priests, protestants, presby-
> ters, independents, Anabaptists, and to all sorts of
> sects and sectaries whatsoever: This [is] unto you
> all, to prove or disprove the doctrine of the Quak-
> ers, which is the same with Christ, the apostles,
> and prophets, which does prove your doctrine to
> be false and out of the doctrine of Christ.

Your testimony, which you (who are called Christians by
name) do bear of the coming of Christ, is only the letter of
the scriptures, because that there are records left of Christ's
words which He spoke in the Mount, which He spoke at Jerusalem, at Samaria, which He preached among the multitude,
and [there are records of] the many miracles that He wrought,
what He spoke to the soldiers when He was apprehended, what
He spoke before the High Priest and Pontius Pilate, and what
He spoke when He was upon the cross. The disciples having
written of His preaching, of His miracles that He wrought, and
of His sufferings, those writings are your testimony of Christ.
Again, the apostles (after they had received the Holy Ghost and
power from above when Christ was offered up and ascended),
the apostles having received His eternal Spirit, and they going
on in the work of God, converted thousands to the faith and did
great and wonderful works and miracles by the Spirit of Christ
which they had received. They traveled up and down in several
parts of the world and turned people from darkness to the light,

and from the power of Satan unto God. There was a record of their works, service, and actions which is called the Acts of the Apostles, which does testify of several remarkable works, actions, and conversations that were wrought by them through the eternal Spirit. After they had gathered several churches and people into the unity of the eternal light and Spirit of God, and had begotten many into the faith, which could bear witness in the Spirit of God of the eternal truth, which they had received through the doctrine of the Spirit.

The apostles, when they were separated and at a distance from those churches, wrote several epistles to the saints that were gathered, sanctified in Christ Jesus, and made partakers of the precious faith, and such as were called to be saints. The apostles wrote not their epistles to the world, nor to such as were not gathered by them, neither Jews nor Gentiles, but to the churches of Christ, sanctified in Christ Jesus, called to be saints, of what sort or denomination so ever they were, or went under, whether Corinthians, Ephesians, Romans, Galatians, etc.

Now the apostasy and darkness coming over, the false apostles getting up, being erred and gone from the Spirit and turned aside from the life and power, of the purity and innocency that the apostles were in, and turning out of the light of the glorious gospel which was in them, the darkness came over them. The antichristian spirit entered in amongst them for the apostle John saw in his time that the antichrist was come and entered into the world, whereby he said, he knew it was the last time and that there were many antichrists already. He knew it was the time that Christ had prophesied of, that false prophets should come in sheep's clothing, but inwardly were ravening wolves, ravened and erred from the spirit of truth which was in the true apostles, and so did deceive many that even darkness covered the face of the earth and all was lost. The beast rose out of the sea and out of the earth and all the world wondered after them, fell down, and worshiped the beast and antichrist and his power. So all nations were made drunk with his cup of fornication and abomination.

Yet this was not unseen nor undiscovered before it came, for Christ prophesied of it: that false christs and antichrists would come in the later days, wolves in sheep's clothing would come, and by their fruits you should know them (Matt. 7:15). The apostle Paul knew that grievous wolves would enter in among them after his departure, that would not spare the flock (Acts 20:29). Peter was sensible of false prophets that were among the people, and did also foretell of false teachers that should privily bring in damnable heresies, even denying the Lord that bought them. He also saw that many would follow their pernicious ways and that, through covetousness, they with feigned words would make merchandise of people. Paul saw, in his epistle to Timothy, that in the last days perilous times should come, that men should be lovers of themselves, having a form of godliness, but denying the power. "Avoid such people," says the apostle, for of these sort are they which creep into houses (calling them churches) and lead captive silly women, laden with sin, and led away with divers lusts, ever learning, and never able to come to the knowledge of the truth. Now as Jannes and Jambres withstood Moses, so do these [men] also resist the truth: men of corrupt minds reprobate concerning the faith (2 Tim. 3:1-8). Again, the same apostle says, "...the time is coming when people will not endure sound teaching, but having itching ears they will accumulate for themselves teachers to suit their own likings, and will turn away from listening to the truth and wander into myths" (2 Tim. 4:3-4).

All these seeing that this apostasy would come, this is a certain testimony that it was to come, is come, and has overspread the face of the earth since the apostles' days—as has been clearly manifested by the many heads and horns of the beast and of the dragon, and the many religions and sects that have started up since the days of the apostles, and as one got up, another was pulled down. Now the blind people, that have been nursed up in blindness, darkness, and ignorance under this cloud of apostasy, when the truth is manifested and risen through this darkness and apostasy and they, seeing that the scripture speaks of false prophets, say the false prophets are but come now. They call the Spirit of truth the false prophet, because it bears testimony against the false worships in the world.

But, I would ask such people, which of these sects or heads or horns that have been set up since the days of the apostles, which of them they look upon to be the true prophets? Whether it is the pope, Luther, or Calvin? Or which other of the old fathers (so called), or bishops and presbyters, independents, and Anabaptists? All these have been, have had their time in this apostasy, and have gotten the writings of the prophets, Christ and the apostles, and so have all had the form of godliness, but some of them denied the power of godliness—according to the prophecy of the apostle Peter, who said there were false prophets among the people, even as there should be false teachers among them which should bring in damnable heresies and that they should receive the reward of unrighteousness, who have forsaken the right way and are gone astray following the way of Balaam who loved the wages of unrighteousness. [They were those], the apostle Jude said, whose mouths must be stopped, who subvert whole houses, teaching things they ought not, for filthy lucre's sake, who serve not the Lord Jesus Christ, but their own bellies and count gain godliness.

Let all people search and read who these are, whether these are the true prophets or the false? Whether these have not been, and yet are, in the time of apostasy? All Christendom (as it's called) had had the scriptures and professed Christ from the declaration thereof, not from the Spirit of truth in themselves, but because they have heard that there was such a man who died at Jerusalem and that there were such men after Him as the apostles were. They, having their words and writings upon record, do make these a sufficient testimony for them of their knowledge and worship of God, and so preach, teach, take texts out of these words, add thereunto their own inventions, and so feed poor ignorant people with these. Here has been the worship that has been upon the face of the earth all the time of the dark night of apostasy since the apostles' days.

Let any honest, reasonable heart judge whether this can be a sure ground and true testimony for people (to trust their souls under such) for teaching? It was not the apostles' practice to take others' records and writings, that had been spoken from others, but they spoke as the Spirit gave them utterance and as the Holy Ghost taught them, not with wisdom of words, but in the demonstration of the Spirit and of power. Yet they will bring a scripture and say, Christ took a text, "The Spirit of the Lord God is upon me, because he has anointed me to preach good news to the poor. He has sent me to proclaim release to the captives" (Luke 4:18; see also Isa. 61:1). When He had read these words, He closed the book and said, "Today this scripture has been fulfilled in your hearing," (Luke 4:21), for it was He that the prophet spoke of, who is the anointing and the anointed, to preach glad tidings to the poor, liberty to the captive, and to the opening of the blind eyes. But these blind leaders lead the blind, but do not open their eyes, though they make the scripture a covering for their false worship. Let anyone prove and try the teachers themselves. They are as blind, as ignorant of their own souls, and as far from having a true testimony of assurance of their own salvation, as those they speak to or pretend to teach. Let people consider this, seriously lay it to heart, and beware how they trust their souls under such teachers and teaching, who have no other nor better testimony than records without them, which were given forth from the Spirit of God in others, which Spirit is eternal and infallible, which these teachers of the world cannot in truth confess, but must (if they confess truth) utterly deny that they have any such Spirit, as many of them have done already. How can these be true teachers of people in the way of truth, which have not the Spirit of truth? For if it be not an infallible spirit, it is a lying spirit, and not the Spirit of truth.

Now let the people seriously consider what they venture their souls upon, for it is not a deceitful lying spirit that will feed the soul. It is the Spirit of life and truth that nourishes the soul and leads into all truth. Here is the chief difference between them and us: they have the words and declaration of Christ and the apostles, declared from the Spirit of life; we have the Spirit which these words were declared from. Not another, but the same eternal Spirit which they had, do we witness and bear our testimony of: the same Christ (and not of another) which witnessed a good confession before Pontius Pilate and was crucified upon the cross of Jerusalem. This Christ, which all the Christians in Christendom profess in words, do we bear testimony of in the Spirit of life and power, according to the scriptures.

It may be objected and said, "How came you to this Spirit, seeing that you say darkness and apostasy have been over the face of the earth since the days of the apostles and that all worships and professions have been but from the letter of scriptures without them? This is but an upstart religion. How is it that you are attained to this that none are attained to in so many hundred years before? Are you wiser than all our forefathers? What is become of all that is gone before?"

This objection is against the unlimited Spirit and power of the living God, who did foresee the apostasy before it came. Christ and the apostles did prophesy of it. The same objection might be against the Lord, when He said unto Pharaoh, I even for the same purpose have raised you up, that I might show my power in you, and that my power might be declared throughout all the earth. Therefore He has mercy on whom He will have mercy, and whom He will He hardens. You will say then unto me, why does He yet find fault? Who has resisted His will? Nay, but oh man! Who are you that replies against God? Shall the thing formed say to Him that formed it, why have you made me thus? What if God, willing to show His wrath and to make His power known, endured with much long suffering the vessels of wrath fitted to destruction, that He might make known the riches of His glory on the vessels of mercy which He had before prepared unto glory. This is the very case. The Spirit of the Lord cannot be limited, but limits all according to the good pleasure of His will, that He may make His power known.

Furthermore, as to our particular, we answer, we received not this Spirit of man, nor by man, but by the immediate power and revelation of Jesus Christ, according to the work and operation of it in us. The apostle said, when it pleased the Lord to reveal his Son in the apostle, he consulted not with flesh and blood, but went on in obedience unto the Lord. So, the same Spirit that revealed the Son in the apostle revealed Him in us, for we neither received it of man, neither were we taught it by man, but by the revelation of Jesus Christ. No man could teach it to us, but who had the revelation of Jesus Christ, according as the apostle said to the Romans, "If the Spirit of Him who raised

Jesus from the dead dwells in you, he who raised Christ Jesus from the dead will give life to your mortal bodies also through His Spirit which dwells in you" (Rom. 8:11). Again, "Do you not know that you are God's temple and that God's Spirit dwells in you?" (1 Cor. 3:16). Though these scriptures bear testimony to the truth of this, yet these scriptures are not our testimony only, for we have our testimony in the same Spirit as was in them that spoke forth the scriptures. These scriptures bear testimony with us, and we to them, and so are in unity with the same Spirit which gave them forth.

This is the hope that we are to give an account of to everyone that asks with meekness and fear, for God has made known unto us the riches of the glory of this mystery amongst the Gentiles, which was Christ in them (and now in us), the hope of glory. This is the same Christ which was offered up at Jerusalem once for all, through the eternal Spirit. This is the hope which purifies, even as He is pure, which hope makes not ashamed, but anchors the soul upon the rock, Christ Jesus. The apostles who had the eternal Spirit are our examples. This is not an upstart religion which we are of, but a pure religion and undefiled before God, which keeps every one that keeps in it, unspotted of the world. Yet, this has been hid from ages and generations past, but now is revealed unto us by the Spirit, which Spirit people have erred from in the time of the apostasy. From this, they do err at this very day and such count the Spirit within heresy and go to scriptures without men and traditions of men, and teach those for doctrine. Here is the reason wherefore this Spirit and revelation have been hid so many hundred years, even because people have been erred from the Spirit of God in them, through which the revelation is manifested. They have been erred in their hearts. Therefore, the way of God has not been known.

Christ said to the woman of Samaria when He was on the mountain where Jacob's well was, where the Jews used to worship, (He said), they worshiped they knew not what. He also said the time was coming that they should not worship in Jerusalem (which was a place commanded of God for the Jews to worship in) nor in this mountain. He further testified that God was a spirit and that they that worshiped Him, must worship Him in Spirit and in truth, saying, the Father was seeking such to worship Him, for they only are the true worshipers of God.

Now I do ask all the teachers and professors in Christendom, where this Spirit is, that God is to be worshiped in, if it be not in man? How it is or can be attained to, any otherwise than by the light of Christ Jesus, with which He has lighted every man that comes into the world, in whom is life and this life is the light of men? Where this worship of God in the Spirit is performed, if it be not in man? Where God's throne is, where the Ancient of Days does sit? Where the scepter of Christ is swayed, which is a righteous scepter? Where the King is that shall reign and prosper, whose name is called, the Lord our Righteousness? How and where must people come to worship God in the Spirit, who deny the light of Christ to be their leader and teacher, and say it is natural. Some say everyone has it not. Others say it is not sufficient. So they are all upon heaps and in confusion, who believe not in the light which Christ Jesus has enlightened them withal, who is the light of every man. So [in] denying the light, and being erred from it, [they] are in darkness until now, stumble, and know not whither they go.

Christ says, "I am the light of the world; he who follows me will not walk in darkness, but will have the light of life" (John 8:12). Again, he says, "while you have light, believe in the light, that you may become sons of light" (John 12:36). "I have come as light into the world, that whoever believes in me may not remain in darkness" (John 12:46). Now I do ask any of the teachers of the world, how any comes to see Christ any otherwise than by the light, seeing that He said to the Jews who talked with Him and He with them, they had not heard His voice, nor seen His shape, for He whom God has sent, they believed not.

This may be the condition of the priests of the world and teachers of the letter. They ought to own it, that they have neither heard His voice at any time, nor seen His shape. How should they, when they deny the light of Christ that is in them to be their guide and teacher—which Christ has lighted them withal, which is the key of David which opens and none shuts, and shuts and none opens? He told the Jews, that they did search the scriptures that did testify of Him and in which they did think to have eternal life, but, He says, "You refuse to come to me that you may have life. I do not receive glory from men." He says, "But I know that you have not the love of God within you. I have come in my Father's name, and you do not receive me; if another comes in his own name, him you will receive. How can you believe, who receive glory from one another and do not seek the glory that comes from the only God?" (John 5:39-44). This He spoke to the Jews, that He said had not His word abiding in them, yet they searched the scriptures, who did not believe in Him. Though He did many miracles among them, yet they persecuted Him, sought to kill Him, and took up stones to stone Him, who is given for a covenant to the people and for a light to the Gentiles, that He may be the salvation to the ends of the earth.

This is the new and everlasting covenant, the promise of God the Father, who has said, is it a light thing that you should raise up the tribes unto Jacob and restore again the preserved of Israel? With whom the Lord has said, I will make a new covenant, I will write my law in their hearts and put my Spirit in their inward parts [a composite paraphrase of Isa. 49:6 and Jer. 31:33]. By this Spirit and light does God teach His people Himself. All that come to the leading and teaching of this Spirit come to the knowledge of the Lord, which shall cover the earth, even as the waters cover the sea. To this light did the apostle [Paul] turn people from the darkness, and from the power of Satan unto God. By the nature of this divine light, did the Gentiles see the things contained in the law, which showed the work of the law (of the Spirit) written in their hearts, their consciences also bearing witness in the day when God shall judge the secrets of men by Jesus Christ, according to the Gospel. Here the apostle does justify the Gentiles, in that he says, not the hearers of the law are justified, but the doers, and their uncircumcision, which did the law, he accounted circumcision. [He] said to the Jews, shall not their uncircumcision judge your circumcision which breaks the law? He further says, we are the true circumcision who worship God in the Spirit, rejoice in Christ Jesus, and have no confidence in the flesh, for he is not a Jew that is one outward. Neither is that circumcision which is outward in the flesh, but he is a Jew who is one inwardly. That is circumcision that is of the heart, in the Spirit, and not in the letter, whose praise is not of men, but of God (paraphrase of Romans 2). This is the seal of the everlasting covenant that takes away the foreskin of the heart and washes away the filth of the flesh. Here the knowledge of the true God is manifested in man, where God shows it unto him, according to the apostle's doctrine (Rom. 1:9).[1]

When Paul came to Mars Hill and saw the Athenians' altar, with the inscription upon it to the unknown God, he said, "The God who made the world and everything in it, being Lord of heaven and earth, does not live in shrines made by man, nor is He served by human hands, as though He needed anything, since He Himself gives to all men life and breath and every-thing. And He made from one every nation of men to live on all the face of the earth, having determined allotted periods and the boundaries of their habitation, that they should seek God, in the hope that they might feel after Him and find Him. Yet He is not far from each one of us, for, "In Him we live and move and have our being..." (Acts 17:24-28). Here the apostle did not lead them out to the writings and records of others with-out them, but he brought them to Him in whom they did live, move, and had their being, that so they might feel after Him and find Him. He said, "He is not far from each one of us," and he brought them off the outward temple which was made with hands. [He] said to the Corinthians,[2] "you are God's temple." As God says, I will dwell in them and walk in them, "and I will be their God, and they shall be my people." "If any one destroys God's temple, God will destroy him. For God's temple is holy, and that temple you are." "Do you not know that your body is a temple of the Holy Spirit within you, which you have from God? You are not your own; you were bought with a price. So glorify God in your body."

Here the apostle clearly demonstrates that the bodies of God's people are His temple. God is the Spirit that is in them. This is the teacher and preacher, which the apostle turns and brings people to, whom he teaches. He told the Romans, "The righteousness based on faith says, Do not say in your heart, 'Who will ascend into heaven?' (that is, to bring Christ down) or 'Who will descend into the abyss?' (that is, to bring Christ up from the dead). But what does it say? The word is near you, on your lips and in your heart (that is, the word of faith which we preach)," says the apostle (Rom. 10:6-8). *Mark:* "But how," he says, "are men to call upon Him in whom they have not believed? And how are they to believe in Him of whom they have never heard? And how are they to hear without a preacher?... So faith comes from what is heard, and what is heard comes by the preaching of Christ" (Rom. 10:14, 17). This is the word which the apostle preached, which is nigh, in the heart, which word opens the blind eye and unstops the deaf ear. They cannot hear without this word of faith, by hearing of which, faith comes; none can hear without this preacher, who is sent to bring glad tidings of good things. But this is not the preachers of the letter of the scriptures without them, for they have preached many hundreds of years, but the deaf ears are not unstopped yet, nor the blind eyes opened by their preaching. So the scripture is now fulfilled, which the prophet Isaiah spoke of, who said, "Bring forth the people who are blind, yet have eyes; who are deaf, yet have ears!" (43:8). Again, he says, they have eyes and see not; ears and hear not; hearts and do not understand.

The Lord says, "I will lay waste mountains and hills, and dry up all their herbage; I will turn the rivers into islands, and dry up the pools. And I will lead the blind in a way that they know not, in paths that they have not known I will guide them. I will turn the darkness before them into light, the rough places into level ground" (Isa. 42:15-16). Them that come into this path and way must come from the blind teachers of the world, who are leaders of the blind, [who] keep people in blindness and ignorance of God and His truth, who deny the light to be a sufficient teacher, which is the eye of the whole body. But with this eye they do not see. Neither can they believe the truth, if it be declared unto them, except they come to the light that does manifest it in them. Now the apostle Peter directed those that he wrote to, unto "the prophetic word made more sure" (2 Pet. 1:19) than that which he heard in the mount, (see Matt. 17:1-

5), which word was a word of prophecy, whereunto (he said) they did well that they took heed, as unto a light that shined in a dark place, until the day dawned and the day-star arose in their hearts. This is the testimony of Jesus, which is the spirit of prophecy. But the teachers of the world say, it is the scripture that the apostle speaks of.

Let any that have but common reason judge whether the apostle was like to say, that the scriptures were a more sure word than the voice of God that was heard in the mount, which said, "This is my beloved Son, with whom I am well pleased; listen to Him," and that the scriptures should be a light shining in a dark place, that the scriptures should be the day dawning and the day-star raising in the heart. If people would but look into things, they might see their deceitfulness, for the apostle goes on with these words, saying, "First of all you must understand this, that no prophecy of scripture is a matter of one's own interpretation, because no prophecy ever came by the impulse of man, but men moved by the Holy Spirit spoke from God" (2 Pet. 1:20-21). Here the apostle dissuades them from looking at the scriptures to be of any private interpretation, or coming by the will of man, which is their whole work, to give their meanings and interpretations in their own wills unto [scripture], which is wholly contrary to the apostle's exhortation and doctrine, who said, "we did not follow cleverly devised myths when we made known to you the power and coming of our Lord Jesus Christ, but we were eyewitnesses to His majesty" (2 Pet. 1:16). The apostle Paul, who was raised up by the power, Spirit, and voice of the Lord who said, "…rise and stand upon your feet; for I have appeared to you for this purpose, to appoint you to serve and bear witness to the things in which you have seen me and those in which I will appear to you, delivering you from the people and from the Gentiles—to whom I send you to open their eyes, that they may turn from darkness to light" (Acts 26:16-18). [The] apostle goes on, bearing his testimony, having obtained the help of God, "testifying both to small and great, saying nothing but what the prophets and Moses said would come to pass: that the Christ must suffer, and that, by being the first to rise from the dead, He would proclaim light both to the people and to the Gentiles" (Acts 26:22-23). This was the witness and the testimony which the apostle held forth, who was a minister of God. But these teachers of the world deny and gainsay this doctrine. The apostle says, "Therefore, having this ministry by the mercy of God, we do not lose heart. We have renounced disgraceful, underhanded ways; we refuse to practice cunning or to tamper with God's word, but by the open statement of the truth we would commend ourselves to every man's conscience in the sight of God. And even if our gospel is veiled, it is veiled only to those who are perishing. In their case "the god of this world has blinded the minds of the unbelievers, to keep them from seeing the light of the gospel of the glory of Christ, who is the likeness of God" (2 Cor. 4:1-4). See here and behold how the apostle recommended himself to every man's conscience in the sight of God. Yet his gospel might be hid to them that were lost, were from the light, and would not believe, which the god of this world had blinded their minds, lest the light should shine unto them. So it is the same still.

Our gospel is hid unto such as believe not in the light: for God, who commanded the light to shine out of darkness, "has shone in our hearts to give the light of the knowledge of the glory of God in the face of Christ" (2 Cor. 4:6). If our gospel is hid, it's hid to them that are lost. Again, he says, "...you were darkness, but now you are light in the Lord; walk as children of light," for all things that are reproved, are made manifest by the light, wherefore he says, "Awake, O sleeper, and arise from the dead, and Christ shall give you light" (Ephesians 5). This is the message which the apostle [John] did declare, "that God is light and in him is no darkness at all. If we say we have fellowship with him while we walk in darkness, we lie and do not live according to the truth; but if we walk in the light, as he is in the light, we have fellowship with one another, and the blood of Jesus his Son cleanses us from all sin" (1 John 1:5-7). This is the message of the minister of God. The apostle gave thanks unto God the Father, who had made them meet to be partakers of the inheritance with the saints in light, who had delivered them from the power of darkness and [who] had translated them into the kingdom of His dear Son.

This is not a new doctrine, though it may seem so to many, because this mystery has been hid and the Spirit of God, which opens this mystery, erred from and turned from by those that have been teachers of people—and not only so. Even their doctrine has been and now is that none must look for nor expect revelation, nor inspiration by the Spirit of God. So they do what in them lies to stop this current of life and spirit, which Christ Jesus, the fountain of all life, has set open, who in the last day of the feast, "stood up and proclaimed, If any one thirst, let him come to me and drink. He who believes in me, as the scripture has said, 'Out of his heart shall flow rivers of living water'" (John 7:37-38). This He spoke of the Spirit, which these teachers of the world would stop, the pourings of which Spirit is unlimited to son or daughter, Jew or Gentile, barbarian, Scythian, bond or free, time or place, or condition, but according to the good pleasure of His will, who is the author and fountain of it. All that are ministers of God and of the Spirit, it is their joy and desire that people grow into the light of life, for they that are in the light, the day of destruction shall not overtake them as a thief, who are children of the light and of the day. This is the desire of all the faithful in Christ Jesus, that they dwell and abide in the light, where the fellowship is one with another, and where the power of God preserves and keeps from the pollutions of the world and temptations of Satan, which power is made manifest "through the appearance of our Savior Christ Jesus, who abolished death and brought life and immortality to light through the gospel" (2 Tim. 1:10), whose immortality dwells in the light, where the Lord God Almighty and the Lamb is the temple. Here the city comes to be known, which "has no need of sun or moon to shine upon it, for the glory of God is its light, and its lamp is the Lamb. By its light shall the nations walk; and the kings of the earth shall bring their glory into it…. But nothing unclean shall enter it, nor anyone who practices abomination or falsehood, but only those who are written in the Lamb's book of life" (Rev. 21:23-24, 27).

This is the great work which the Lord is working in this His day and the spiritual building which He is rearing and setting up. He has put His hand to work. When He works, who can let it? Who has resisted His will? Who has directed the Spirit of the Lord, or been His counselor, or taught Him? Of whom took He counsel? Or who instructed Him, taught Him knowledge, and showed Him the way of understanding? Behold, the nations are but as the drop of a bucket, and as the small dust of the balance before Him. He takes the isles as a very little thing. Lebanon is not sufficient to burn and the beasts thereof for a burnt-offering. It is He that sits upon the circle of the earth. The inhabitants thereof are as grasshoppers. By His spirit, He will remove the great mountains of the earth. They shall become a plain. He will bring forth the head stone and lay it a-top of all, for the stone which is cut out of the mountain without hands breaks in pieces the image and will become a great mountain. His kingdom, which shall never be destroyed (and shall not be left to other people, but will break in pieces and consume all kingdoms): this is arising. The Ancient of Days is coming to sit in judgment in the saints of the Most High. The kingdoms of the world are becoming the kingdoms of the Lord and of His Christ. The little one shall become a thousand and the small one a great nation (Daniel 7). The Lord of Hosts will hasten it in His time. So it is in vain to stand against the God of Heaven or resist His work which He has begun in the earth, which He is working and will work by His Spirit in this His day of power. He will make all His people willing and subject to Him. Every knee must bow to Him and every tongue confess to God: for the first Adam was made a living soul, but the second is the Lord from heaven, a quickening Spirit, which does quicken and raise up the just unto the resurrection of life. He is made manifest in His people to destroy the works of the devil which he has wrought in the disobedient man and so brought the first Adam into the fall and under the curse, that the very earth is cursed for his sake. But Christ Jesus, who the apostle saw, made a little lower than the angels, for the suffering of death, has wrought the redemption of man to bring him into a blessed, happy, and perfect condition (Heb. 2:9). All those that believe on Him, trust in Him, obey Him, and wait for Him: Unto them shall He come the second time without sin unto salvation—though the priests and teachers of the world make it their work to destroy this work of redemption of the Son of God who redeems out of sin and all evil, and from vain conversation, to serve the living God in the newness of the Spirit (and not in the oldness of the letter); who redeems from the earth, from the pollutions of the world, and from all unrighteousness.

But this is a mystery which cannot be believed by the dark, ignorant, sinning, and transgressing ministers and professors of the nations, who lie wallowing in their sins and uncleanness and drink up iniquity as the ox drinks water. These that are filling up their measure of iniquity and are wholly covered with the power of darkness, these cannot see how it is possible that ever any should get out of this state and condition, being that they are quite ignorant of their Redeemer living in them. So [they] go about to persuade all people of the impossibility of being freed from sin, but that they must sin all the days of their lives. So [they] keep people in the fall, in the transgression, under the curse, and death is the reward of sin. These ministers are the ministers of death.

But Christ Jesus redeems from under the curse and from under the bondage of sin and corruption which all the creation has long groaned under and awaits for the blessed liberty of the sons and children of God. Glory and honor be unto His holy name forever, who has sent His only begotten Son in the likeness of sinful flesh, and for sin, condemned sin in the flesh. As by one man's disobedience many were made sinners, so by obedience of One shall many be made righteous. This the disobedient will never know, who turn from and disobey the Holy One that should make them righteous.

Here are all the priests, teachers, and professors of the world, in the disobedience, erred from the Spirit, in the transgression, and in sin. So [they] teach all people to be sinners, as they can do no otherwise, who are not ministers of the light of Christ nor turn people to the light of Christ in whom is no sin, who has said, "unless one is born of water and the Spirit, he cannot enter the kingdom of God" (John 3:5). Now that which is born of the Spirit is Spirit and this enters the kingdom. "It is the Spirit that gives life, the flesh is of no avail; the words that I have spoken to you," says Christ, "are spirit and life" (John 6:63). But there were some that believed not. Now those that deny the light of the Spirit of life, they know little of the pourings forth of the Spirit or of the manifestation of the Spirit of God, which He has given to everyone to profit withal. But the ministers of darkness, which have erred from the Spirit and endeavor to keep all people back from the teaching, leading, and guiding of the Spirit: they do not profit with it, but hide their talent in the earth and count the Lord a hard master. Therefore, he must needs take it from them and give it unto those that have profited with it. This is witnessed, manifested, and seen with those that have eyes in this day. The apostles spoke as the Spirit gave them utterance. Their preaching was not with the enticing words of man's wisdom, but in the power and demonstration of the Spirit, not according to the wisdom of the world. [They] spoke the wisdom of God in a mystery, even the hidden wisdom which God had revealed unto them by His Spirit, which Spirit searches all things, yea the deep things of God.

Therefore, it is good for everyone to have a true testimony of this eternal Spirit, which believes not every spirit, but tries them, whether they be of God, and proves all things, and holds fast that which is good. He that lays his foundation here, he builds not his house on the sand, but on the rock, on which the whole church is built, which is in God, the Father of our Lord Jesus Christ, and [the] pillar and ground of truth. When the wind blows, the storms and the tempests beat, this house will stand: for they that are joined to the Lord are one spirit with Him and of one heart and soul. If they were ten thousand, they are all one, and all of one, who are begotten, born, brought forth, and sanctified by one Spirit. Here is the mystery of the fellowship of the gospel, which is in the unity of the Spirit, which is the bond of peace.

This is not a shadow, not a vanishing, fading thing, but this is a substance that proceeds from the living God and returns to Him, by which Spirit He is made known unto the sons of men and by which Spirit He works and creates in Christ Jesus unto righteousness and true holiness. By one Spirit we are all baptized into one body, who have been made to drink all into one Spirit, whether Jews or Gentiles, bond or free. If they come into this Spirit which makes, unites, and knits together, they are all one, for the body is not one member, but many. But they that deny this Spirit, and the teaching thereof, are not of this body, nor do [they] drink of this cup of the New Testament. They are drinking of the cup of fornication and idolatry, for the apostle [Paul] said they could not sit at the Lord's table and the table of devils. They could not drink the cup of the Lord and the cup of devils [see 1 Cor. 10:21f]. So they that drink not of the cup of the Spirit (new) in the kingdom, let them read in their own bosoms what they are drinking of.

The apostle [Paul] said that the Corinthians were manifestly declared to be the epistle of Christ [see 2 Cor. 3:1-4] ministered by Him, written not with ink, but with the Spirit of the living God, not in tables of stone, but in the fleshly tables of the heart. Here is the ministration manifested by them that are ministers of the Spirit of the living God, who reach unto that of God in the hearts of people. The same Spirit in people answers to the anointing which is in them, which they received, even the unction of the Holy One. Such need not that any man should teach them, but as the same anointing teaches them, which is truth, and no lie (see 1 John 2:26f). This is not the ministration of the letter, but of the Spirit, for the letter kills, but the Spirit gives life (see 2 Cor. 3). The apostle [Paul] was made an able minister of the New Testament, whose ministration was more glorious than the law, which was written in tables of stone. He says the Lord is the Spirit, which Spirit is written in the fleshly tables of the heart. Where the Spirit of the Lord is, there is liberty. All that are the sons of God are led and guided by the Spirit of God (see Romans 8). According to the apostle's words, "because you are sons, God has sent the Spirit of his Son into our hearts, crying 'Abba! Father!'" (Gal. 4:6). We through the Spirit wait for the hope of righteousness by faith (see Gal. 5:5).

Who walks and abides in the Spirit does not fulfill the lusts of the flesh, for the flesh lusts against the Spirit, and Spirit against the flesh, and these are contrary the one to the other. This is the teacher, leader, and guide of God's people, who are called to be saints and sanctified in Christ Jesus through the obedience of the Spirit which subdues, brings down, and subjects under in man and woman that which is contrary. It [is] working and operating in the inward man, putting on and adorning the heart with a meek and quiet spirit, which is with the Lord of great price. This is precious in the sight of the Lord. When the Spirit beautifies with salvation and sanctifies the heart to the Lord by its powerful working, here the Lord is glorified in his saints. This eternal Spirit, substance, and Word "is living and active, sharper than any two-edged sword, piercing to the division of soul and spirit, of joints and marrow, and discerning the thoughts and intentions of the heart" (Heb. 4:12). This is the sure teacher that lays a true foundation on which the prophets and apostles are built, the cornerstone, which all the wise builders have disallowed and set at naught, which is now become the head of our corner (glory and honor be to the Highest for ever), according to Christ's words, who said, "Have you never read in the scriptures: 'The very stone which the builders rejected has become the head of the corner; this was the Lord's doing, and it is marvelous in our eyes'? And he who falls on this stone will be broken to pieces; but when it falls on any one, it will crush him" (Matt. 21:42, 44). Peter says, "...it stands in scripture: 'Behold, I am laying in Zion a stone, a cornerstone chosen and precious, and he who believes in Him will not be put to shame.' To you therefore who believe, He is precious, but for those who do not believe, 'The very stone which the builders rejected has become the head of the corner,' and 'A stone that will make men stumble, a rock that will make them fall'; for they stumble because they disobey the word, as they were destined to do" (1 Pet. 2:6-8).

This is the stone and word that all the disobedient stumble at, Jews and Gentiles that will not come to the light which Christ Jesus (who is the light of men) has enlightened them withal. The obedience of the light of Christ Jesus is the obedience to the cross of Christ, the preaching of Him crucified (the apostle [Paul] says), "a stumbling-block to Jews and folly to Gentiles, but to those who are called, both Jews and Greeks, Christ the power of God and the wisdom of God" (1 Cor. 1:23-24). The light, the power of God, the cross of Christ, the apostle did not preach with the wisdom of words, lest the cross of Christ should become of no effect, which is unto all that are saved, the power of God. He says, "for since, in the wisdom of God, the world did not know God through wisdom, it pleased God through the folly of what we preach to save those who believe" (1 Cor. 1:21).

This is the wisdom of God, the way of God, not to teach people by that which man's wisdom teaches, that which man's dark heart invents, imagines, and studies out of his brain, but by that which the Holy Ghost teaches in this His day in which He is risen in His eternal Spirit. They that can believe in this foolishness of preaching are saved. They that cannot believe, to them this gospel is hid, because that the foolishness of God is wiser than men and the weakness of God is stronger than men, who has said, "I will destroy the wisdom of the wise, and the cleverness of the clever I will thwart" (1 Cor. 1:19). God has chosen the foolish things of the world to confound the things that are mighty, that no flesh might glory in His presence, but in Him. This is the will, way, and work of the Lord, by which He teaches people. So they have access by one Spirit unto God the Father, Jews and Gentiles, barbarians, Scythians, bond and free, if they come unto Christ Jesus the light, life, and everlasting covenant who is given to be the salvation unto the ends of the earth, who was offered up by the Eternal Spirit once for all (see Eph. 2:18).

All people who come unto this eternal Spirit which is in them, of what sort so ever, if they come to this light, covenant, and Spirit, they are all one in Christ Jesus. If they be Christ's, then are they *Abraham's* seed and heirs according to the promise. All that do endeavor to keep the unity in the Spirit and bond of peace are strengthened by this Spirit in the inner man. The eyes of their understanding come to be enlightened. They do come to comprehend with all saints, the height, the breadth, and the depth of the love of God, which passes knowledge. [It] is a mystery to the wise rabbis of the world and all the disobedient ones that will not stoop to the light of Christ, His power and cross in them, but will live in the liberty of the flesh, where they may exercise their fleshly liberty, pride and ambition, superfluity of naughtiness, vain glory and arrogancy, voluptuousness, pomp and vanity of the world—all which are of the first man, fallen from God and of the earth, earthly. The cross of Christ, which is the power of God, is to crucify the affections and the lusts thereof, the world, the flesh, and the devil.

[Those] who are obedient and faithful to the witness and testimony of the living God in them, and to its guiding, leading, and teaching, put off the old man and his deeds and put on the new man, Christ Jesus, who is created after God in righteousness and true holiness, and so come to be renewed in the spirit of their minds, to have their consciences cleansed, and their bodies washed with pure water (see Ephesians 5). So they bring forth the fruits of the spirit, which are in all, goodness, righteousness, and truth: yes, love, joy, peace, long-suffering, gentleness, faith, meekness, and temperance. Against such there is no law. Who are in this state keep the law, break it not, and are in the love which fulfills it, and one with the justice, equity, and righteousness of it (which[3] was added because of transgression). Where there is no transgression, there is no law. The law is not against such.

But we find little of those fruits of the Spirit in the world (which cannot receive the Spirit of truth) among all professors, priests, and teachers thereof. This is the mark which Christ has set us to try the false prophets by. He says, by their fruits shall you know them, who get the sheep's clothing (the scriptures), but inwardly are ravening wolves. We have found the priests, professors, and teachers of these nations to minister persecution and cruelty to us, as the prisons and gaols of these nations may bear (and have borne) testimony. Another mark that Christ gave of the false prophets, to know them by, was when all men should speak well of them, for so did their fathers of the false prophets. Now let all people judge, whether this be not the condition of the priests and teachers at this day, for they bear rule by their means. Yet the people love to have it so. But what will they do in the end thereof, when God comes with his overflowing scourge, breaks the covenant with death and the agreement with hell, and sweeps away the refuge of lies (see Matthew 7). Many hundreds of years have been their strength, but God is coming to overturn them, to confound them, and to cut down the fruitless trees that bring not forth good fruit and do manifest that the evil tree cannot bring forth good fruit. Men do not gather grapes of thorns, nor figs of thistles, for the best of them have been but as a briar and the most upright of them as a thorn hedge—as many will come to see when their eyes come to be opened. They shall be as a bowed wall and as a tottering fence (see Psalm 62). Let but the honest and the godly hearted judge between them and us, whether their fruits are not the fruits of the flesh, which the apostle [Paul] says are these: adultery, fornication, uncleanness, lasciviousness, idolatry, witchcraft, hatred, variance, emulation, wrath, strife, seditions, heresies, envyings, murders, drunkenness, revilings, inordinate affections, evil concupiscence, covetousness which is idolatry, anger, malice, blasphemy, filthy communication, effeminateness, and abusers of themselves with mankind, revelings, banquetings, excess of wine, and abominable idolaters, filthiness, foolish jesting and talking, which are not convenient (see Gal. 5:19-21; Col. 3:8; 1 Cor. 6:9-10).

Let the upright judge, whether they be not "lovers of self, lovers of money, proud, arrogant, abusive, disobedient to their parents, ungrateful, unholy, inhuman, implacable, slanderers, profligates, fierce, haters of good, treacherous, reckless, swollen with conceit, lovers of pleasure rather than lovers of God, holding the form of religion but denying the power of it." From such (the apostle exhorts the people to) turn away (see 2 Tim. 3:2-4).

Now the reader may judge it to be harsh or censoriousness in charging all these fruits of the flesh upon the teachers and ministers of the world, many of which they would seem to evade. But this I say further for the information of the reader: that they are ministers of darkness, and not ministers of the light, but deny the light both to minister from, and to minister to. The ministers of God were ministers of light. The message they brought was, "God is light and in him is no darkness at all" (1 John 1:5). Paul was made an able minister of the New Testament, not of the letter, but of the Spirit. He turned people from the darkness to the light, and from the power of Satan unto God who is light, in which whosoever walks, the blood of Jesus Christ His Son cleanses him from all sin.

Now these ministers and teachers of the world, whose ministry stands in the darkness where all sin is committed and all the fruits of the flesh acted: these cannot clear themselves from these things before mentioned, for they stand in that ground which brings forth the fruits of the flesh. Therefore is their doctrine for sin and against perfection and cleansing. [They] preach frequently that none can be free from sin while they are upon the earth: for they are guilty in their hearts and consciences that they sin continually. So with their blind dark minds they can never see that any can be cleansed or redeemed from sin, which is wholly contrary to the apostle's doctrine, which says that Christ was manifest to take away sin. Whosoever abides in Him, sins not. Whosoever sins has not seen Him, neither known Him. He that commits sin is of the devil; whosoever is born of God does not commit sin, for His seed remains in him. He cannot sin, because he is born of God. In this are the children of God manifest and the children of the devil (paraphrase of 1 John 3:1-10). Now, reader, do but in soberness weigh these things according to the truth of the scriptures. This will take away the prejudice and remove the objection which might arise in your mind concerning the fruits of the flesh applied to the teachers and professors.

All that desire after godliness and the truth as it is in Jesus, they must turn from them that have the form, and deny the power, who bring forth the fruits before mentioned, for as many as receive Christ Jesus (the light), to them He gives power to become the sons of God. It is the word of His power by which all things were created, by which He upholds all things. It is His power that brings His seed out of bondage and out of the house of darkness. The gospel of our Lord Jesus Christ, which the apostle was not ashamed of to preach, is the power of God unto salvation, unto every one that believes, to the Jew first and also to the Greek. This treasure the apostle had in an earthen vessel that the excellency of the power might be of God. Here was the apostle's doctrine established: in the mighty power of God, whereof (says he) I was made a minister according to the gift of the grace of God given unto me, by the effectual working of His power, that so I might know the power of His resurrection and the fellowship of His sufferings.

But this is a mystery and unknown to the teachers and ministers of the letter, who are in forms and appearances without the power, in the ordinations of men, and receive their approbations only from men, and are made ministers by men. These deny and resist the power and Spirit the apostles were made ministers of, even deny immediate revelation, say it is ceased, and so deny the gift of God's grace which has appeared unto all men to teach the denying of ungodliness, and all wordly lusts, and (all that obey it and follow it) to live godly, righteously, and soberly in this present evil world. So those teachers endeavor to limit the Spirit of the living God to times and persons, which cannot be limited, and say we must not look for it now, as in the apostle's time. We must look to the scripture and not to the Spirit for revelation. So [they] blaspheme the God of Heaven, gainsay His truth and the revelation of the Son of God, who said the Father was a spirit and they that worship Him must worship Him in Spirit and in Truth. He was seeking for such worshipers to worship Him, and has said, there is none that knows the Son, but the Father; neither does any man know the Father, save the Son, and he to whom the Son reveals him.

So these teachers, that deny revelation and the Spirit's teaching, do not desire that the Son should be known by the

Father's drawing, for there is none that can come to the Son, except the Father draw him. Neither is it possible for them to bring people to the knowledge of the Father, who deny revelation, being there is none that knows the Father, save the Son, and he to whom the Son reveals Him. So the infinite mercy and wisdom of the Lord God has hid these things from them and has revealed them unto the faithful and obedient who walk in His light and keep in it where the revelation is manifested. Christ Jesus saw great cause of thanking the Father, the Lord of heaven and earth, that He had hid those things from the wise and prudent and had revealed them unto babes—children of the light who were begotten into the light, were translated into it, made one with it, and abode in the anointing which they received in the beginning. They had fellowship with the Son and with the Father. He that believes on the Son has everlasting life; he that believes not on the Son shall not see life, for the Father loves the Son and shows Him all things that He does. For as the Father raises up the dead and quickens them, even so the Son quickens whom He will. Who believes in the light, and walks in the light of the Son of God, is quickened by Him and has the Father revealed to him, not in parables, but He does show him plainly of the Father. He has committed all judgment to the Son, that all men might honor the Son, as they honor the Father. He that honors not the Son, honors not the Father that has sent Him. He that believes not in the light of the Son of God, he honors not the Son. He whose mind is not turned unto the light of God in him, he knows not the Son, nor Him that sent Him. "Jesus cried out and said, 'He who believes in me, believes not in me but in Him who sent me. And he who sees me sees Him who sent me. I have come as light into the world, that whoever believes in me may not remain in darkness'" (John 12:44-46). Mark here now, Christ's words: He that sees Him to be the light come into the world sees Him that sent Him. He that believes in Christ, that is come a light into the world, believes on Him that sent Him. He that believes on Christ Jesus, who is come a light into the world, abides not in the darkness, but has the light of life.

This is the great work of God, that every one believe on Him that God has sent. He that believes in Him has the witness and testimony of Him in himself. He that knows not that Christ is in him is a reprobate. This is the will of Him that sent me, (says Christ), that every one that sees the Son may have everlasting life, and I will raise him up at the last day. This is the portion and reward which the true believers receive from Him who is the resurrection and the life. He that believes on Him, though he was dead, yet shall he live and he that lives and believes shall never die. (He that can receive it, let him.) Jesus says, no man comes unto me, except the Father, which has sent me, draw him. It is written in the prophets, (says He), they shall be all taught of God; every man therefore, that has heard and has learned of the Father, comes unto Me (paraphrase of John 11:25-26).

Here now, everyone, whose eye is single, may see that none can come, but whom the Father draws and they that are taught of God, come to the Son, who He has given a light into the world. This is the way, the truth, and the life, and no man comes to the Father but by Him. In no other way nor by no other name under heaven shall anyone be saved, but by Him. He is able to save to the utmost all those that come unto God by Him. No other foundation can any man lay than this which is already laid. But let everyone take heed how he builds thereon. He which preaches another gospel, let him be accursed: for this is the rock and foundation on which the whole church is built, Christ Jesus the light and precious stone which Jews and Gentiles that are saved are built on, for He is their peace, who has

made both one and has broken down the middle wall of partition which was between. Through Him we have both an access
to the Father and are built upon the foundation of the apostles
and prophets. Jesus Christ Himself is the chief cornerstone, in
whom all the building fitly framed together grows unto a holy
temple in the Lord, who are built together for a habitation of
God through the Spirit. Here is the great work of the mystery
of God, which He is working in this His day, whose tabernacle
is with men, and the most High dwells in the kingdoms of men.
He whose delight is with the sons of men is arisen, and wisdom
lifts up Her voice and cries, "To you, O men, I call, and my cry
is to the sons of men. O simple ones, learn prudence; O foolish
men, pay attention" (Prov. 8:4-5).

Christ Jesus is coming to reign. The scepter of His righteousness, which is a right scepter, will He sway the nations
with. Those [of] His enemies, that will not that He should reign
must even be broke, bound, and slain before Him. Therefore, it
is good for all people to hear His voice, to turn at His reproof,
to hearken diligently to the Word that is nigh in the heart, and
to incline their ears that their souls might live. There is a Word
that says, "this is the way," which way is for the wayfaring
man. This teacher will never more be removed into a corner,
but their eyes must see their teacher. This way, which has long
been hid and hedged up, has the Lord now opened and made
manifest in this His day. The law and the testimony, which were
sealed among the disciples, are now opened. The Word, which
is the light, is now revealed. The light is shining in the consciences of men and they that are children of light and of the
day walk in it. It shines in their hearts and gives them the light
of the knowledge of the glory of God in the face of Jesus Christ,
the express image of the invisible God, the first-born of every
creature. This cleanses and purges the conscience from dead

works to serve the living God. In this every one may draw near in full assurance of faith, having their hearts sprinkled from an evil conscience and their bodies washed with pure water.

It was impossible that the blood of bulls and goats should take away sin, but this Man, after He had offered one sacrifice for sin, sat down at the right hand of God, expecting till His enemies be made His footstool. The high priests, that went before Him, were daily offering the same sacrifice, which could never take away sin, nor make perfect as appertaining to the conscience. Yet, by one offering, Christ Jesus the everlasting high priest, has perfected forever them that are sanctified. This is He that does the will of God, who said, "Lo, I have come to do thy will, O God, as it is written of Me in the roll of the book" (Heb. 10:7), by which will we are sanctified, whereof the "Holy Spirit also bears witness to us; for after saying, 'this is the covenant that I will make with them after those days, says the Lord: I will put my laws on their hearts, and write them on their minds;' then He adds, 'I will remember their sins and their misdeeds no more'" (Heb. 10:15-17). Here the apostle witnesses the Holy Ghost to be the witness and testimony of God's truth in the promise of the new covenant, of the law written in the heart, and of the Spirit being put in the inward parts.

These, that deny the Spirit of God, which gives testimony and witness of His everlasting covenant, are strangers to this life and aliens to the commonwealth of Israel. The covenant of the promise is to the elect seed of Abraham, not of the bond woman, but of the free; not of the seeds, which are many, but of one, which is Christ, that is elect, according to the foreknowledge of God the Father, through sanctification of the Spirit, unto obedience, and sprinkling of the blood of Christ, who does purify their souls in obeying the truth, through the Spirit. For this cause is the gospel preached, that they may be judged according to men in the flesh, but live according to God, in the Spirit. This is the chief end of the ministry of the gospel, which is glad tidings to the poor, liberty to the captive, but judgment to him that has captivated the seed, till that be dead which has held the seed in bondage and till the enmity be slain, the middle wall of partition taken away, and of twain made one new man. This is the ministration of the everlasting gospel. Christ also has once suffered, being put to death in the flesh, but quickened in the Spirit, by which also He went and preached unto the spirits in prison. He that is anointed to preach glad tidings to the poor, and liberty to the captives, is now preaching to the spirits in prison, binding up the broken-hearted, and raising up them that are fallen. He is enlightening the blind eyes, unstopping the deaf ears, opening the prison doors, and bringing the prisoners forth of the prison houses, so that the prisoners of hope do rejoice, that have been in the pit, which is without water. Christ calls, come unto me, every one that is weary and heavy laden. They shall find rest for their souls, who will take His yoke upon them, which is easy, and His burden, which is light, to the obedient and to the faithful who are subjected unto him and wait for Him—they that love Him and keep His commandments, who says, he that has my commandments and keeps them, he it is that loves me. He that loves me shall be loved of my Father and I will love him and will manifest myself unto him.

Here is an infinite reward, which will even satisfy the immortal soul, which nothing can satisfy but the living God. Christ says, if any man loves me, and keeps my words, my Father will love him. We shall come unto him and make our abode with him. Here the Comforter, which is the Holy Ghost, which proceeds from the Father and the Son, is manifested, which does teach all things and bring all things to remembrance. This is the inheritance which the saints in light are made partakers of, even the Spirit of truth, which the world cannot receive, which leads into all truth all them who obey and follow the leading, guiding, and teaching of it. The apostle desired that Timothy might know how he ought to behave himself in the house of God, which is the church of the living God, the pillar and ground of truth. Without controversy, (says He), great is the mystery of godliness, God manifest in the flesh, justified in the spirit, seen of angels, etc. This mystery I have endeavored in part to open, according to the scriptures. If any come to the key of David,[4] which opens this mystery, they will see the truth of it and seal to it in that measure of the spirit which God has given to everyone to profit withal: for unto every one of us is given grace, according to the measure of the gift of Christ, according to the good pleasure of His will. He that is faithful in the little, is made ruler over much. So this is the way, the truth, and the life. Every one that does set at naught this, and resists it, let his blood be upon his own head.

Now let the reader, by what is here written, seriously examine, and try by the scriptures, and the measure of the Spirit of God, who are the true prophets and the false, who are the true teachers and who are the false, and what is the true worship of God and the false. Let him venture his soul, as he dare answer before a just and righteous God.

> From a true lover of the souls
> of all people who desires the good
> of all, and that all might come
> to the knowledge of the truth.

Margaret Fell

CHAPTER 2

A DECLARATION OF QUAKER PRINCIPLES AND PRACTICE FROM MARGARET FELL TO KING CHARLES AND PARLIAMENT, JUNE 1660

Historical Introduction

The events that led to Margaret Fell's *Declaration* included not only the re-establishment of the monarchy in England, but also the troubled times immediately preceding it. In 1658, the military dictatorship of Oliver Cromwell had all but reached its end. Support for the religious Commonwealth established by civil war and regicide in the 1640s had eroded to a shadow of its former substance as the 1650s progressed. As it declined, the regime made increasingly desperate attempts to convey an image of legitimacy by covering itself with royal trappings and prerogatives and by accelerating the persecution of enemies, real and suspected. George Fox witnessed the tenor of these times as recorded in his *Journal*:

> And great sufferings we went through in these times of Oliver Protector and the Commonwealth, and many died in prisons. And they have thrown into our meetings wild fire and rotten eggs, and brought in drums beating, and kettles to make noises with; and the priests as rude as any…have beat and abused Friends. (353)

After the death of Cromwell on September 3, 1658, the political and social climate deteriorated toward disintegration. Richard Cromwell proved a weak successor to his strongman father, and the nation swam with plots and rumors of plots. The Quakers found themselves not only suspect by the national regime, but also quick prey for their many enemies among the clergy and magistrates on the local level whose hatred and violence had been restrained in the past by the authority and strength of the central government.

The re-establishment of the monarchy and the return to the throne of Charles II, while presenting real hope for a cessation of these extended and bitter persecutions, did not bring immediate relief. Even as Charles entered England in May, 1660, George Fox was being arrested by overzealous constables during a visit to Margaret Fell's estate at Swarthmoor. Many other Friends experienced similar suffering. The invasion of Fell's house on the weakest of pretexts (a search for arms), the seizure of Fox, and his imprisonment in Lancaster under the accusation of plotting against the King, galvanized her to more formidable work and activity than she had ever before been involved.

At the age of forty-six, she began the arduous journey to London (200 miles south) to foster good will with the new government and to seek a remedy for the persecutions of Quakers throughout the nation. She could not foresee that she was entering upon one of the most active and significant decades of her ministry, a decade that would see the initial success of her mission followed by some of the most distressing persecutions of Friends. She, herself, would know four years as an estateless, imprisoned, legal non-person in the eyes of the government, but as her "Relation" (see p. 167 and note, p. 225) attests, the sufferings neither cowed nor slowed her. Seeking religious toleration in the first days of Charles' reign, she would again be in London pursuing the same purpose at his death in 1685.

Fell's *Declaration and Information from the People Called Quakers...* reflects her key position among early Friends and her stature as one of the individuals best suited to represent them before, and negotiate with, the government. Her profound faith, her extensive knowledge of the Gospel, her articulateness in expressing it, and her utter clearness and firmness about what Friends could not grant to the government made her a natural for the task—a task little short of monumental.

Her task proved nearly overwhelming. Although she was able to gain Fox's release by September of 1660, a stunning blow befell her general effort in January, 1661, when the Fifth Monarchy Men rose in London against the government. In the general suspicion and turmoil that followed, 4,230 Friends were swept into prison by their enemies. Of these were 270 Swarthmoor Quakers imprisoned without warrant or examination, most for refusing the Oath of Allegiance. It would be September, 1661, before Fell could turn homeward after having received assurances from King and Council that the thousands of Quakers in prison would be freed.

Her fifteen months had been consumed with extraordinary activity: audiences with King and Council, meetings with persons of notable weight and influence in the Court, the production of requested papers and documents, the refutation of misrepresentations (including lingering memories of the Nayler Affair), attendance at religious Meetings, extensive correspondence not only with Friends but also with their supporters and detractors, the strengthening of imprisoned Quakers in the midst of suffering for their faith—even a painful correspondence advising her daughters at Swarthmoor Hall who were struggling to keep the estate running and attempting to fend off efforts by the local magistrates to destroy the Swarthmoor Meeting. The work of representing Friends and interpreting their faith was a formidable one.

Content Introduction

The *Declaration* is a particularly important document. It is the first public statement of the Quaker peace testimony, preceding by six months its more famous sister, the January 1661 *Declaration from the Harmless and Innocent People of God called Quakers, Against All Plotters and Fighters in the World*. The content of Fell's *Declaration* can easily be separated into six areas: (1) an explanation of the source of the persecution Friends had suffered to date, (2) a thorough review of the religious and scriptural basis behind those aspects of the Quaker witness that most seemed to challenge the authority of the government, (3) a simple request for civil rights and religious toleration, (4) a brief declaration of the essence of the Gospel, (5) a demonstration that the Quakers were true and trustworthy, and (6) a prophetic warning to the Crown to rule with justice and mercy.

The *Declaration* actually had two purposes. The first and most obvious to the modern reader was simply to inform a new government of the movement's principles and practices. The second is a striking reflection of the fact that early Friends believed they must be forthright, frank, and clear in representing their faith to the world. Thus, this second purpose of the *Declaration* is to fulfill the Quaker responsibility to be clear and truthful with all men and women so that ignorance, misunderstanding, and misinformation might not foster bloodshed and persecution. Fell emphasizes that a Quaker failure to declare and inform would be wrong and make the movement responsible for the violence done to it.

Fell proceeds to review the source of the persecution that has pursued Friends since their appearance in the 1650s. She identifies that source as religious, not political, noting that the movement has suffered under all the king's enemies, from a persecution akin to that which pursued the apostles in their declaration of Truth.

However, while Fell emphasizes the religious origins of the persecution, she clearly understands that three common actions among Quakers have usually been misinterpreted as attacks on the authority of the state, thus begetting political suppression. These three actions were refusal to support the state church with mandatory tithes, refusal to swear or take Oaths including those of Allegiance, and refusal to show special signs of respect to people of higher class or station. For observing these three testimonies, Quakers suffered their greatest persecution. The clergy, threatened with financial loss, was notably malicious and violent. Government officials suspected at least contempt, at worst treason, when Friends refused to swear and do obeisance to authority. Aristocrats raged at being addressed similarly as the common people. This is why Fell uses the initial third of the *Declaration* to explain in detail the true foundation of these testimonies in Christ's teaching and the honest motivation from which they spring. She has rightly anticipated the issues that would be of most immediate concern to the new government in establishing respect for its authority.

The actual petition within the *Declaration* is so simple that modern readers may wonder why it was not immediately granted. What Friends sought were only their "civil rights and liberties of subjects, as freeborn Englishmen," and religious toleration to worship as they would. The restoration of rights might be expected as part of the normal requirements of English Law—requirements that had too often been ignored at the height of social unrest, hysteria, and persecution.

However, the request in 1660 for religious freedom was no easy matter to grant. Charles II had just returned to a nation that had executed his father in a religiously inspired civil war, a nation with a large Protestant majority wary of Roman Catholicism, horrified by religious persecution raging on the Continent of Europe and deeply suspicious that the new monarch had serious Catholic preferences.

If an Act of Toleration would be granted it would, of course, cover more than Quakers and might serve the cause of Catholic subversion of the country. In short, toleration meant danger. Religion would be the great frustration of Charles' reign and the downfall of his successor.

From the petition, Fell moves to a distillation of the Gospel, stressing the worldly harmlessness of the people that embrace it and who walk in that Light and Spirit which takes away the occasion for strife and war. And here she makes one of her most telling arguments for toleration of the Quakers. The worldly politician in Charles would obviously be concerned with whether he could trust them. The answer was simple. What men and women have stood steadfastly for the principles and practices of their faith, in spite of the very worst persecutions? The Quakers. While other churches twisted, turned, compromised, plotted, and subverted their way from one change of government to the next, only Friends had been steady and predictable. Given Charles' own knowledge of the mercurial sectarians that had claimed his father's head, this was one of Fell's strongest arguments.

The last three pages of the *Declaration* announce the peace testimony of Friends. In a passage that might be termed the essence of that witness, Fell carefully sets forth the Quaker concept of the Lamb's War, a *spiritual* war with evil. As obedient followers of Christ, Quakers believed themselves involved in a cosmic struggle against evil in all its forms, both in their own hearts and in the world. This struggle could only be fought with spiritual weapons to gain a victory that could only be won as Christ won it, through suffering, so the all-conquering power of God might be manifest. While this war had many social dimensions (some of them already set forth in the *Declaration*), the heart of the struggle was the mission to bring all humanity to an inward knowledge of Christ so they might learn of His will and be directed by His Spirit into the way of peace.

The prophetic Christianity of early Friends determined the tone of the entire *Declaration*. Prophetic even in style, the document was straightforward, frank, and plain—uncharacteristic of the verbal inflation and embellishment that usually found their way into documents of this genre. Fell, herself, notes the difference: "This we do in the presence of the Lord declare, not in flattering titles, but in reality and in truth of our hearts...." Nowhere is there a fawning word. In fact, like the Old Testament prophets, Fell feels compelled to warn: "Now you have come into the throne to be tried. We cannot but warn you in your day 'to do justice, and to love kindness.'" Of course, Friends offer no worldly threat to back up the warning. God will be the judge and for Fell that was enough. Already, in her lifetime, she had seen the demise of governments, the fall of kings, protectors, and magistrates. For her, the power of God was a present and reliable reality.

The Declaration

A Declaration and an Information from Us, The People Called Quakers, to the Present Governors, The King, and Both Houses of Parliament, and All Whom It May Concern

This was delivered into the King's hand, the 22nd day of the Sixth Month, 1660, by M.F.[1]

We are the people of God called Quakers, who are hated and despised and everywhere spoken against as people not fit to live, as they[2] were that went before us who were of the same spirit, power, and life and were as we are, in that they were accounted as the offscouring of all things, by that spirit and nature that is of the world (1 Cor. 4:10-13). So the scripture is fulfilled, he that is born of the flesh persecutes him that is born of the Spirit (Gal. 4). We have been a suffering people under every power and change, and under every profession of religion that has been and borne the outward power in the nation these twelve years, since we were a people. Through the Old Enemy which has continually appeared against us, not only in the profane people of the nation, but also in the highest profession of sorts and sects of religion, we have suffered under, and been persecuted by them all: even some persecuted and imprisoned till death, others their bodies bruised till death, stigmatized, bored through the tongue, gagged in the mouth, stocked, and whipped through towns and cities, our goods spoiled, our bodies two and three years imprisoned, with much more that might be said, which is well known to the actors thereof.

This [was] done, not for the wronging of any man, nor for the breach of any just law of the nation, nor for evil-doing, nor desiring any evil, or wishing any hurt to any man, but for conscience's sake towards God, because we could not bow to their worship, and because we could not maintain a ministry, which ministry we could not join with nor own. So we look upon it to be unjust to maintain them. We receive nothing from nor trust our souls under their teaching, who teach for hire and divine for money, which the prophets of the Lord cried woe against. Christ said a hireling was a thief and a robber, and would fly because he was a hireling (John 10:7-13). They are maintained by tithes, contrary to Christ and the apostle's doctrine, which said the priesthood was changed that took tithes, and the law also that gave them (Heb. 7:1-12), and which witnessed Christ Jesus to be the everlasting offering once for all, which says, "for it is fitting that we should have such a high priest, holy, blameless, unstained, separated from sinners, exalted above the heavens" (Heb. 7:26). "In the days of His flesh, Jesus offered up prayers and supplications, with loud cries and tears, to Him who was able to save Him from death, and He was heard for His godly fear. Although He was a Son, He learned obedience through what He suffered: and being made perfect He became the source of eternal salvation to all who obey Him" (Heb. 5:7-9). For obedience to Him and His commands, who said, "Do not swear at all," do we suffer (Matt. 5:34-35; James 5:12, 2:10).[3] He said, call no man master upon earth, for you have one master in heaven; and [He] has said, how can you believe [who] seek honor one of another, and not the honor that comes from God only? He has said, "Let what you say be simply 'Yes' or 'No'; anything more than this comes from evil" (Matt. 5:37).

[We suffer] because we cannot respect persons,[4] [respecting] which is contrary to the apostle's doctrine and practice, who has said, "Truly I perceive that God shows no partiality, but in every nation anyone who fears Him and does what is right is acceptable to Him" (Acts 10:34-35; Matt. 22:16). The apostle James exhorted his brethren, "Show no partiality as you hold the faith of our Lord Jesus Christ, the Lord of Glory…. But if you show partiality, you commit sin, and are convicted by the law as transgressors" (James 2:1, 9). Contrary to this faith and doctrine we are made transgressors by the powers of the earth, because we cannot respect persons, commit sin, and be made transgressors of the law of God.

This has been the only ground and cause of our sufferings, because we obeyed the command of Christ, the author of our eternal salvation, and observed the apostle's doctrine and practice. Not for any other cause or end have our sufferings been, but for conscience's sake, because we cannot bow to men's wills and worships contrary to the command of Christ Jesus, our everlasting priest, king, and prophet, whom we serve with our spirits and worship in that which the world calls heresy (Acts 24:14 KJV).

Now, because several of you who are most concerned in this government are not acquainted with our principles and practices, neither have known our innocency and sufferings, and [because] the Old Enemy by whom we have suffered, at this time is ready to incense, and instigate, and infuse secretly into the minds of them who are strangers to us, against whom we have not transgressed, we do not desire to give any just occasion of offense to those present governors, who yet have not done us much wrong, in making any law against us that we know of, and we do believe would not, if you did rightly understand our innocency, integrity, nakedness, and singleness in our carriage towards all men upon the face of the earth; if you would but examine and search out our carriage and behavior towards all men's souls, persons and estates; if these things were searched out and examined through the nations and that no prejudice were let into your minds from others' words which proceed from secret envy, malice and hatred, and not from any just ground they have against us, but as it is from a contrary spirit and mind. As it was in the Jews against Christ and in all others against the apostles, so it is the same now against us.

This we commit to the Lord who will plead our cause and clear our innocency, who has said, "Vengeance is mine and I will repay it."[5] Now that they know we cannot swear, nor take an oath for conscience's sake, but have suffered because we could not take them: now do the magistrates of several counties of the nation (through the suggestion of the priests' envy, which is inveterate against us) tender us an oath, which they call The Oath of Allegiance with several other engagements, what their own wills can invent,[6] on purpose to ensnare us, that upon the denial thereof they may cast us into prison (and have already cast several of us into prison) at their pleasure.

We do therefore declare (to take off all jealousies, fears, and suspicions of our truth and fidelity to the King and these present governors) that our intentions and endeavors are and shall be good, true, honest, and peaceable towards them; that we do love, own, and honor the King, and these present governors, so far as they do rule for God, and His truth, and do not impose anything upon peoples' consciences, but let the gospel have its free passage through the consciences of men, which we do not know that they have (by any law) as yet imposed. If they grant liberty of conscience towards God and towards man, then we know that God will bless them, for want of which has been the overthrow of all that went before them. We do not desire any liberty that may justly offend any one's conscience, but the liberty we do desire is that we may keep our consciences clear and void of offense towards God and towards men, and that we may enjoy our civil rights and liberties of subjects, as freeborn Englishmen. This we do in the presence of the Lord declare, not in flattering titles, but in reality and in truth of our hearts, and shall manifest the same. Now that we may be clear in the presence of the living God and of all just and moderate men, that they may not have their hands in blood and persecution as those have had that are gone before, and that they may not be ignorant of us and of our principles and practice, and so receive information against us from others' envy, which may be contrary to our very principles and the truth as it is in Jesus: Therefore, that we may be free from the blood of all men (Acts 20:26), and that they may not have a hand in persecuting and oppressing the innocent, whose cause God has pleaded and will plead, we do therefore inform the governors of this nation high and low: we are a people that desire the good of all people, and their peace, and desire that all may be saved, and come to the knowledge of the truth, the way, and the life which is Christ Jesus, the everlasting covenant, who is given for a light to the Gentiles and to be the salvation to the ends of the earth (1 Tim. 2:1-4; Acts 16:25f; Rev. 21:24; 1 Cor. 4).[7]

All the nations of them that are saved must walk in this light of the glorious gospel, which has shined in our hearts and given us the light of the knowledge of the glory of God in the face of Jesus Christ. To this light we direct peoples' minds, that everyone in particular may have a teacher and testimony according to the righteousness of faith, which speaks on this wise [matter], "The word is near you, on your lips and in your heart" (Rom. 10:8). If everyone would come to this, there would be a feeling of our intents to be just, innocent, and righteous, and God's justice and righteousness, who has said, "Then

I will draw near to you for judgment; I will be a swift witness against the sorcerers, against the adulterers, against those who swear falsely…" (Mal. 3:5).

Now if [all] would turn to this witness in their own consciences, this would keep from oppressing and persecuting of others without cause, for God is coming to teach His people Himself, by His own light and Spirit, who has said, "It is written in the prophets, and they shall be all taught by God" (John 6:45)—which many of us now do witness, for which cause are we persecuted. "All your sons shall be taught by the Lord…. In righteousness you shall be established; you shall be far from oppression…" (Isa. 54:13-14).

The testimony that we have born has been chiefly against the priests, teachers, and professors of these nations, that are out of the life and power, for when it pleased the Lord to reveal His Son to us, we saw them to be absolute deceivers of the people and betrayers of their souls, for they lead them wholly from that of God in them, to the letter of the scripture without them and to their own inventions, imaginations, and meanings which they speak, who are not taught of God themselves. For all their high profession, there is scarce one of them that dares say they have the infallible Spirit of God, the same as the apostles had, that gave forth the scripture. The apostle says that which may be known of God is manifested in them, for God shows it unto them. No people can retain God in their knowledge, and worship Him as God, but first they must come to that of God in them. But these teachers deny this doctrine, have manifested themselves several ways to all sober-minded people to be men not fearing God, and are not true to their principles, for [people] who have minded them and seen their carriage and behavior in all these changes (which have been many, as may be further manifest) that have been these eight years.

There have been changes of governments, of Parliaments and Protectors—several in these eight years—and all these have been warned not to uphold these priests contrary to peoples' consciences, but that everyone might have their liberty: that they that would have them might maintain them, and they that could not receive their doctrine might not be forced to maintain them. But this would not satisfy their covetous practice. They went on in the way of cruelty, persecuting and oppressing the innocent, casting into prison, took treble damages, spoiled their goods, and made havoc of poor peoples' increase and fruits of their labors. Neither would the magistrates hear, but suffered them to go on in their persecution and upheld them by a law to the oppressing of the innocent, until the Lord by His mighty power overturned them and broke them one after another. Those priests turned to every power and every government, as it turned: made petitions, addresses, and acknowledgments to every change of government; conformed to every power for their own ends; and showed much love and zeal to every present power for their own ends, though many of them were instruments to throw others out. Through their deceit and subtleties, [they] have kept themselves in, in all these times and changes.

Now let any honest hearted people judge whether these be found principled men that can turn, conform, and transform to every change according to the times. Whether these be fit men to teach people. Their fruits are manifest. God does discover them more and more, that they cannot proceed much longer. Their folly is so much made manifest, they have used their utmost endeavors to cause persecution to continue upon us. But, the Lord has seen it. We commit all to Him and can freely say, "Lord, do not hold this sin against them" (Acts 7:60). But for the bearing [of] our testimony against them for the deceiving and betraying of poor ignorant people that are blind and led by them that are blind into a ditch (Matt. 15:14), we cannot but in pity and love to peoples' souls bear our testimony against them. Therefore have our sufferings been because we desire the good of all people and the salvation of their souls. This is all we desire and suffer for, that all might come to the knowledge of the Lord, who said, "...all shall know me, from the least of them to the greatest" (Heb. 8:11).

We are a people that follow after those things that make for peace, love, and unity. It is our desire that others' feet may walk in the same. [We] do deny and bear our testimony against all strife, wars, and contentions that come from the lusts that war in the members, that war against the soul, which we wait for, and watch for in all people. [We] love and desire the good of all. For no other cause but love to the souls of all people have our sufferings been. Therefore have we been numbered amongst the transgressors and been accounted as sheep for the slaughter, as our Lord and Master was, who is the captain of our salvation, who is gone before us, who though He was a Son, yet learned His obedience by the things that He suffered, who said, "My kingship is not of this world; if my kingship were of this world, my servants would fight..., but my kingship is not from the world" (John 18:36). This is He that "came not to destroy men's lives but to save them" (Luke 9:56). This is He that is our Lord and Master, whose testimony we must seal with our blood, if it be required of us. "For though we live in the world we are not carrying on a worldly war, for the weapons of our warfare are not worldly but have divine power to destroy strongholds" (2 Cor. 10:3-4). Our weapons are not carnal, but spiritual,[8] who have given our backs, our cheeks, and our hair to be smitten by all professions out of the life and power, who have done it to purpose (which the Lord has overturned), who were often warned by us, under whom we have undergone cruel sufferings.

Now you are come into the throne to be tried. We cannot but warn you in your day "to do justice, and to love kindness" (Micah 6:8), whereby the violence of the wicked might be stopped, which is for your own good and prosperity. So we desire and also expect to have the liberty of our consciences, just rights, and outward liberties, as other people of the nation, which we have promise of, from the word of a King, that we may not be made a prey upon by the profane envious people and priests [against] whom [and] against [whose] corruptions we have born our testimony—who thirst not only after our estates and liberties but our blood also, who have already begun to search our houses, to apprehend our members, and cast them into prison, there to be kept without bail or mainprize, under pretense as if we were thieves, murderers, or traitors (which they cannot lay to our charge, whereby they endeavor to take away our lives)—who are enemies to no man's person upon the earth.

Treason, treachery, and false dealing we do utterly deny—[and] false dealing, surmising, or plotting against any creature upon the face of the earth. We speak the truth in plainness and singleness of heart. All our desire is your good, peace, love, and unity. This many thousands will seal with their blood, who are ready not only to believe, but to suffer, but only that the blood of the innocent may not come upon yourselves, through false informations.

Given forth the 5th of the Sixth Month, 1660.
Margaret Fell

We, in the unity of the Spirit and members of Christ, do subscribe and witness to the truth of this and in behalf of those in the same unity.

George Fox	Gerrard Roberts
Richard Hubberthorne	John Stubbs
Samuel Fisher	Thomas Coveny
Joseph Fuce	Thomas Harte
Gobert Sikes	James Strut
Amos Stodert	Ellis Hookes
William Caton	

And now I am here to answer what can be objected against us on the behalf of many thousands, who are baptized with one Spirit into one body, to bear my testimony, to be offered up for the service of the faith, and to give an account of the hope that is in me to everyone that asks according to the scripture; [I] who was moved of the Lord to leave my house and family, and to come two hundred miles to lay these things before you, who to the will of the Lord am committed.

Margaret Fell

CHAPTER 3

WOMEN'S SPEAKING JUSTIFIED, PROVED, AND ALLOWED OF BY THE SCRIPTURES...

Historical Introduction

Women's Speaking, first published in 1666, has become one of Margaret Fell's better known pamphlets—perhaps the only one that has received significant attention in the last half of the twentieth century. Feminist historians have recognized it as a key document, one of the first by a woman, in the evolution of woman's vision as an equal partner with man. Some have termed it a "plea" for women's spiritual equality and ministry with men, but a quick glance over its vigorous style reveals that description to be not only inadequate, but inaccurate. Women's Speaking is a vigorous declaration of woman's spiritual equality, denouncing and chiding—at times sarcastically—those who would silence women ministers.

As support for her position, Margaret Fell musters her intimate and extensive knowledge of scripture, not to proof-text her opponents, but to explicate in context the many biblical references, both Old Testament and New, which demonstrate the strong and consistent spiritual and prophetic equality of women. More importantly, the pamphlet soundly reinterprets the Pauline stricture that women keep silent in church, by viewing it in its larger epistolary context.

Certainly, the contents of *Women's Speaking* remain deeply relevant today as the majority of Christendom has yet to come to terms with woman's position in Christ's ministry and kingdom. Yet, while the document is of distinct interest to the modern woman, one caveat is necessary. Margaret Fell's argument solely addresses the issue of spiritual equality. Her vision does not extend to social, economic, or political issues. She is, basically, a woman of the seventeenth century. To expect her to be more, even with her extraordinary vision and spiritual insight, would be a distortion and move her out of time—from the realm of reality to that of fantasy.

Yet, Fell's time also played a distinct part in the birth of the pamphlet. Quaker women ministers were constantly challenged by civil and ecclesiastical authorities. In fact, George Fox had already issued two pamphlets of his own in their defense, one pre-dating Fell's by ten years (1656) and the other by five (1661). *Women's Speaking*, itself, after its first issue in 1666, was reprinted with additional material (beginning page 113) in 1667, and translated into Dutch for publication in Holland in 1668.

Events in the years contiguous to its publication were also influential. In February of 1664, Margaret Fell had been arrested and imprisoned in Lancaster Castle for refusal to take the Oath of Allegiance to the crown. Her subsequent trial that year and her sentence of praemunire in August were to jail her for nearly four years. However, the rigors and stress of these years—which saw the plague of London, the Great Fire of London, great personal discomfort, and loss of her estate—seemed to do little, if anything, to retard her work for Truth. In 1666 alone, besides *Women's Speaking*, she produced in August a lengthy *Epistle to Charles II*, in September the pamphlet *A Touchstone...*, and *The Standard of the Lord Revealed*. In fact, her imprisonment appears to have given her more time for her writing in support of the Gospel, when it stripped her of the more mundane—though equally important—responsibilities she had carried at Swarthmoor Hall as the "nursing mother" of the Quaker movement.

Content Introduction

Fell's care in constructing her argument is readily apparent in the first pages of *Women's Speaking* where she musters her major points, paragraph by paragraph, in her tightly ordered review of the doctrinal and scriptural basis for women's spiritual equality in Christ. The result is a broad picture of the contributions of women to redemptive history and overwhelming evidence that God not only favors women with His Spirit, but that they have played a central role at the most important moments of Divine history. While the Pauline strictures against women speaking in the church are dealt with, Fell rightly places them, first, in the larger context of God's work of redemption and, second, in the full context of the epistles (1 Corinthians and 1 Timothy) in which they appear. Only by setting them in these wider contexts can they be clearly read and properly interpreted.

Fell's key arguments are well worth study in detail. She begins by noting in the very words of Genesis that "God created man in his own image, in the image of God He created him; male and female He created them." Both sexes are clearly part of the image of God. While noting that the serpent chose the woman to approach with his temptation, Fell almost seems ready to question the traditional view that he discerned woman as "the weaker vessel," suggesting that perhaps she was merely "more inclinable to hearken to him." However, as a result of the Fall, God put "enmity between" the serpent "and the woman." Thus, those who oppose women's speaking in the Spirit oppose it "out of the envy of the old serpent's seed," for women now have a special hatred of the Evil One.

From this beginning, Fell reviews the special favor God has shown the female sex through redemptive history: that God calls His church by the name of woman, both in the Old and New Testaments, and that by woman His Son entered the world. Further, Fell notes the special regard of Christ for women, be it the woman of

Samaria, Mary and Martha, Mary Magdalene, or Mary the mother of James. Not only are women received openly and treated as spiritual equals with men, but they also play primary roles in Jesus' resurrection and the proclamation of the Gospel. They are first at the Tomb. They are sent to the disciples to tell them the Good News. Mary Magdalene, herself, is the first to witness Christ risen. As Fell notes with scathing sarcasm, what would have become of human redemption if others had not believed the message brought by these women? They were the ones who were so closely knit to Him in love that they could not depart from the grave "as the men did." She soundly puts away the objections of those who would silence women as the weaker sex, not by arguing women's strength, but by slaying the weaker sex argument with a Christian one: "the weakness of God is stronger than men."

The Pauline strictures against women's speaking are, of course, the key arguments of Fell's opposition. These she approaches on two fronts. First, she reviews the verses in the fuller Pauline context, reviewing many of his other references to women working in the church. Her references indisputably demonstrate that Paul had no problem with *holy* women speaking, women who labored with him in the Gospel. Second, Fell interprets the Pauline strictures as being not against women in general, but against those women yet in the Fall, out of God's Spirit. Women without Christ's Spirit remained under the Law and the Law indeed banned them from speaking. However, women of the New Creation were another matter. To stop their mouths was to stop Christ Himself from speaking, and, of course, it was clear to Fell's readers who would like to quench the voice of Christ. This distinction between the Old and New Creation, the First Adam and the Second (or the First Eve and the Second, if we take the thinking to its logical conclusion) is not an invention for the purposes of Fell's argument, but an essential point of the Christian vision. Though modern scholarship suggests that

Pauline authorship of 1 Timothy is unlikely, that fact does not affect the basic validity of Fell's interpretation. Doctrinally, she remains on firm ground.

Within a year of the pamphlet's publication, Fell found that the necessity of reprinting the paper provided a good opening to add further supporting material to her arguments. She actually added little to the argumentative foundation of the 1666 presentation, but the weight of her new evidence, the devastating blows she deals to her opponents' position, and her terse and effective irony make the section well worth reading as a demonstration of argument well and tellingly made. She reminds us that Paul himself observed that Christ in the male and female is one, that Paul would be contradicting himself if his stricture applied to all women, that women of the New Creation are no longer under the law, and that what women have spoken in the Spirit (as recorded in scripture) constitutes some of the greatest messages of the Bible. Messages even Fell's detractors accept, like Mary's great hymn, the Magnificat (Luke 1:46-55).

Yet, a caveat: While Fell's vision of the spiritual equality of women speaks strongly to our own time, we must not fall into the trap of seeing her as a twentieth century feminist born before her day. As already noted, Fell appears to have accepted some of the traditional seventeenth century English vision of women as the weaker sex, and as individuals who should subordinate themselves to their husbands. To expect her to escape all the biases of her time, to escape influences inculcated since her birth and pervasive and unchallenged in her day, is to deny in her cultural influences which even today influence the sex roles of all of us. To lift Margaret Fell out of her time is to create a deceptive portrait—a portrait of which Fell herself would not approve, for she was a mortal enemy of deceit.

Yet, as we look at her full and long life, she was every bit the equal of the men of her time—in her ministry and travels through England, in her many writings, in her administrative abilities both in the service of her estate and family at Swarthmoor, and in the Quaker movement, in her "diplomatic" service for Truth before the kings of England, and in her sufferings and imprisonments. Just as it is impossible to think of the rise of the Quakers without thinking of George Fox, it is impossible to envision their growth and success in proclaiming the Everlasting Gospel without Margaret Fell.

The Pamphlet

**Women's Speaking Justified, Proved, and Allowed of
by the Scriptures, All Such as Speak by the Spirit and Power
of the Lord Jesus. And How Women Were the First
That Preached the Tidings of the Resurrection of Jesus, and
Were Sent by Christ's Own Command Before
He Ascended to the Father (John 20:17)**

It has been an objection in the minds of many, and several times has been objected by the clergy, or ministers and others, against women's speaking in the church, and so consequently may be taken that they are condemned for meddling in things of God. The ground of objection is taken from the apostle's words, which he wrote in his first epistle to the Corinthians 14:34-35, and also what he wrote to Timothy in the first epistle, chapter 2:11-12. How far they wrong the apostle's intentions in these scriptures we shall show clearly when we come to them in their course and order. First let me lay down how God Himself manifested His will and mind concerning women and unto women.

First, when "God created man in His own image, in the image of God He created him; male and female He created them. And God blessed them, and God said to them, 'Be fruitful and multiply....' And God said, 'Behold I have given you every plant...'" etc. (Gen. 1:27f). Here God joins them together in His own image, and makes no such distinctions and differences as men do, for though they be weak, He is strong. As He said to the apostle, "My grace is sufficient for you, for my power is made perfect in weakness" (2 Cor. 12:9). Such has the Lord chosen, even "what is low and despised in the world, even things that are not, to bring to nothing things that are" (1 Cor. 1:28). God has put no such difference between the male and female, as men would make.

It is true the serpent, that was more subtle than any other beast of the field, came unto the woman with his temptations and with a lie, his subtlety discerning her to be the weaker vessel, or more inclinable to hearken to him, when he said, "when you eat of it [the tree of the knowledge of good and evil] your eyes will be opened," and the woman saw "that the tree was to be desired to make one wise" (see Gen. 3:1-6). There the temptation got into her, and she did eat, and gave to her husband, and he did eat also: so they were both tempted into the transgression and disobedience. Therefore God said unto Adam (who hid himself when he heard His voice), "'Have you eaten of the tree of which I commanded you not to eat?' The man said, 'The woman whom thou gavest to be with me, she gave me fruit of the tree, and I ate.' Then the Lord God said to the woman, 'What is this that you have done?' The woman said, 'The serpent beguiled me, and I ate'" (Gen. 3:11-13). Here the woman spoke the truth unto the Lord. See what the Lord says after He had pronounced sentence on the serpent, "I will put enmity between you and the woman, and between your seed and her seed; he shall bruise your head, and you shall bruise his heel" (Gen. 3:15).

Let this word of the Lord, which was from the beginning, stop the mouths of all that oppose women's speaking in the power of the Lord, for He has put enmity between the woman and the serpent, and if the seed of the woman speak not, the seed of the serpent speaks, for God has put enmity between the two seeds. It is manifest that those that speak against the woman and her seed's speaking, speak out of the envy of the old serpent's seed. God has fulfilled His word and His promise, "when the time had fully come, God sent forth His Son, born of woman, born under the law, …that we might receive adoption as sons" (Gal. 4:4-5).

Moreover, the Lord is pleased, when He mentions His church, to call her by the name of woman, by His prophets, saying, "For the Lord has called you like a wife forsaken and grieved in spirit, like a wife of youth…" (Isa. 54:6). Again, "How long will you waver, O faithless daughter? For the Lord has created a new thing on the earth: a woman protects a man" (Jer. 31:22). David, when he was speaking of Christ and His church, says, "The princess is decked in her chamber with gold-woven robes; in many colored robes she is led to the king, with her virgin companions, her escort in her train. With joy and gladness they are led along as they enter the palace of the king" (Ps. 45:13-15). Also King Solomon in his Song, where he speaks of Christ and His church (where she is complaining and calling for Christ), says, "If you do not know, O fairest among women, follow in the tracks of the flock…" (Song of Sol. 1:8). John, when he saw the wonder that was in heaven, saw "…a woman clothed with the sun, with the moon under her feet, and on her head a crown of twelve stars; she was with child and she cried out in her pangs of birth, in anguish for delivery. And another portent appeared in heaven; behold a great red dragon…. And the dragon stood before the woman who was about to bear a child, that he might devour her child when she brought it forth" (Rev. 12:1-4).

Thus much may prove that the church of Christ is represented as a woman and those that speak against this woman's speaking, speak against the church of Christ, and the seed of the woman, which seed is Christ. That is to say, those that speak against the power of the Lord and the Spirit of the Lord speaking in a woman, simply by reason of her sex, or because she is a woman, not regarding the seed, the Spirit, and power that speaks in her: such speak against Christ and His church, and are of the seed of the serpent, wherein lodges enmity. As God the Father made no such difference in the first creation, nor ever since between the male and the female, but always out of His mercy and loving kindness had regard unto the weak, so also His Son, Christ Jesus, confirms the same thing when the Pharisees came to Him and asked Him if it were lawful for a man to put away his wife. He answered, "Have you not read that He who made them from the beginning made them male and female, and said, 'For this reason a man shall leave his father and mother and be joined to his wife, and the two shall become one'? So they are no longer two but one. What therefore God has joined together, let no man put asunder" (Matt. 19:4-6).

Again, Christ Jesus: When He came to the city of Samaria, where Jacob's well was, where the woman of Samaria was, you may read in John 4 how He was pleased to preach the everlasting gospel to her. When "the woman said to him, 'I know that the Messiah is coming (He who is called Christ); when He comes, He will show us all things.' Jesus said to her, 'I who speak to you am He.'" Also He said unto Martha, when she said she knew that her brother should rise again in the last day, "Jesus said to her, 'I am the resurrection and the life; he who believes in me, though he die, yet shall he live, and whoever lives and believes in me shall never die. Do you believe this?' She said to Him, 'Yes, Lord; I believe that you are the Christ, the Son of God...'" (John 11:25-27). Here she manifested her true and saving faith, which few at that day believed so on Him.

Also that woman that came unto Jesus with an alabaster box

of very precious ointment, and poured it on His head as He sat at meat; it is manifest that this woman knew more of the secret power and wisdom of God than His disciples did, who were filled with indignation against her. Therefore Jesus said, "Let her alone; why do you trouble her? She has done a beautiful thing to me.... And truly, I say to you, wherever the gospel is preached in the whole world, what she has done will be told in memory of her" (Mark 14:3, 9; Matt. 26:6-13). Luke says further, she was a sinner, and she stood at His feet behind Him weeping, began to wash His feet with her tears, and did wipe them with the hair of her head, kissed His feet, and anointed them with the ointment. When Jesus saw the heart of the Pharisee that had bidden Him to his house, He took occasion to speak unto Simon (as you may read in Luke 7) and He turned to the woman, and said [unto] Simon, "Do you see this woman? I entered your house, you gave me no water for my feet, but she has wet my feet with her tears and wiped them with her hair. You gave me no kiss, but from the time I came in she has not ceased to kiss my feet. You did not anoint my head with oil, but she has anointed my feet with ointment. Therefore I tell you, her sins, which are many, are forgiven, for she loved much..." (Luke 7:37-47).

Also, there were many women who followed Jesus from Galilee, ministering unto Him, and stood afar off when He was crucified (Matt. 27:55; Mark 15:40-41). Yea, even the women of Jerusalem wept for Him, insomuch that He said unto them, "Daughters of Jerusalem, do not weep for me, but weep for yourselves and for your children" (Luke 23:28). "And the twelve were with Him, and also some women who had been healed of evil spirits and infirmities: Mary called Magdalene, from whom seven demons had gone out, and Joanna, the wife of Chuza, Herod's steward, and Susanna, and many others, who provided for them out of their means" (Luke 8:1-3).

Thus we see that Jesus owned the love and grace that appeared in women, and did not despise it: and by what is recorded in the scriptures, He received much love, kindness, compassion, and tender dealing towards Him from women, as He did from many others, both in His lifetime and also after [men] had exercised their cruelty upon Him. Mary Magdalene and Mary the mother of James beheld where He was laid: "And when the Sabbath was past, Mary Magdalene, and Mary the mother of James, and Salome, bought spices, so that they might go and anoint Him. And very early on the first day of the week they went to the tomb when the sun had risen. And they were saying to one another, 'Who will roll away the stone for us from the door of the tomb?' And looking up, they saw that the stone was rolled back; for it was very large" (Mark 16:1-4; Luke 24:1-2). They went down into the sepulcher and, as Matthew says, the angel rolled away the stone, and he said unto the women, "Do not be afraid; for I know that you seek Jesus who was crucified. He is not here; for He has risen..." (Matt. 28:5-6). Now Luke says thus, that "two men stood by them in dazzling apparel; and as they were frightened and bowed their faces to the ground, the men said to them, 'Why do you seek the living among the dead? Remember how He told you, while He was still in Galilee, that the Son of man must be delivered into the hands of sinful men, and be crucified, and on the third day rise.' And they remembered His words, and returning from the tomb they told all this to the eleven and to all the rest. Now it was Mary Magdalene and Joanna and Mary the mother of James and other women with them who told this to the apostles; but these words seemed to them an idle tale, and they did not believe them" (Luke 24:4-11).

Mark this, you despisers of the weakness of women, [who] look upon yourselves to be so wise: But Christ Jesus does not so, for He makes use of the weak. When he met the women after He was risen, He said unto them, "'Hail!' And they came up and took hold of His feet and worshiped Him. Then Jesus said to them, 'Do not be afraid; go and tell my brethren to go to Galilee, and there they will see me'" (Matt. 28:9-10; Mark 16:9). John says, when Mary was weeping at the sepulcher, that "Jesus said to her, 'Woman, why are you weeping? Whom do you seek?' Supposing Him to be the gardener, she said to Him, 'Sir, if you have carried Him away, tell me where you have laid Him, and I will take Him away.' Jesus said to her, 'Mary.' She turned and said to Him in Hebrew, 'Rabboni!' (which means Teacher). Jesus said to her, 'Do not hold me, for I have not yet ascended to the Father; but go to my brethren and say to them, I am ascending to my Father and your Father, to my God and your God'" (John 20:15-17).

Mark this, you that despise and oppose the message of the Lord God that He sends by women: what [would have] become [of] the redemption of the whole body of mankind, if it had not cause to believe the message that the Lord Jesus sent by these women, of and concerning His resurrection? If these women had not thus out of their tenderness and bowels of love (who had received mercy, grace, forgiveness of sins, virtue, and healing from Him, [of] which many men also had received the like), if their hearts had not been so united and knit unto Him in love that they could not depart as the men did, but sat watching, waiting, and weeping about the sepulcher until the time of His resurrection, and so were ready to carry His message, as is manifested, how else should His disciples have known, who were not there?

Oh! Blessed and glorious be the Lord. This may all the whole body of mankind say (though the wisdom of man that never knew God is always ready to except against the weak):

"the foolishness of God is wiser than men, and the weakness of God is stronger than men" (1 Cor. 1:25).

In Acts 18, you may read how Aquila and Priscilla took unto them Apollos and expounded unto him the way of God more perfectly, who was an eloquent man and mighty in the scriptures. Yet, we do not read that he despised what Priscilla said, because she was a woman, as many now do.

Now to the apostle's words, which are the ground of the great objection against women's speaking. First, 1 Corinthians 14. Let the reader seriously peruse the chapter and see the end and drift of the apostle in speaking these words. The apostle is there exhorting the Corinthians unto charity, to desire spiritual gifts, and not to speak in an unknown tongue, not to be children in understanding nor to be children in malice, but in understanding to be men. [He says] that the spirits of the prophets should be subject to the prophets, for God is not the author of confusion, but of peace. Then he says, "The women should keep silence in the churches," etc.

It does plainly appear that the women, as well as some others that were among them, were in confusion: for he says, "What then, brethren? When you come together, each one has a hymn, a lesson, a revelation, a tongue, or an interpretation. Let all things be done for edification" (1 Cor. 14:26). Here is no edifying, but confusion speaking together. Therefore he says, "If any speak in a tongue, let there be only two or at most three, and each in turn; and let one interpret. But if there be no one to interpret, let each of them keep silence in the church..." (1 Cor. 14:27-29). Here the man is commanded to keep silence, as well as the woman, when in confusion and out of order.

The apostle says further, "As in all the churches of the saints, the women should keep silence in the churches. For they are not permitted to speak, but should be subordinate, as even the law says. If there is anything they desire to know, let them ask their husbands at home. For it is shameful for a woman to speak in church" (1 Cor. 14:33-35).

Here the apostle clearly manifests his intent. He speaks of women that were under the law and in that transgression as Eve was, and such as were to learn, and not to speak publicly, but they must first ask their husbands at home. It was a shame for such to speak in the church. It appears clearly that such women were speaking among the Corinthians, by the apostle's exhorting them from malice, strife, and confusion. He preaches the law unto them. He says, "In the law it is written, 'By men of strange tongues and by the lips of foreigners will I speak to this people...'" (1 Cor. 14:21 quoted from Isa. 28:11-12).

What is all this to women speaking who have the everlasting gospel to preach, upon whom the promise of the Lord is fulfilled and His Spirit poured upon them according to His Word (see Acts 2:16-18). If the apostle would have stopped such as had the Spirit of the Lord poured upon them, why did he say just before, "If a revelation is made to another sitting by, let the first be silent. For you can all prophesy one by one..." (1 Cor. 14:30-31)? Here he did not say that such women should not prophesy as had the revelation and Spirit of God poured upon them, but women that were under the law, in the transgression, in strife, confusion, and malice. If he had stopped women's praying or prophesying, why does he say, "any man who prays or prophesies with his head covered dishonors his head, but any woman who prays or prophesies with her head unveiled dishonors her head..." (1 Cor. 11:4-5)? "Judge for yourselves; is it proper for a woman to pray to God with her head uncovered?" ("Nevertheless, in the Lord, woman is not independent of man nor man of woman; for as woman was made from man, so man is now born of woman. And all things are from God") (1 Cor. 11:11-13).

[Let us turn to] that other scripture, in 1 Timothy 2, where he is exhorting that prayer and supplication be made everywhere, lifting up holy hands without wrath and doubting. He says in the like manner also, "that women should adorn themselves modestly and sensibly in seemly apparel, not with braided hair or gold or pearls or costly attire but by good deeds, as befits women who profess religion. Let a woman learn in silence with all submissiveness. I permit no woman to teach or to have authority over men; she is to keep silent. For Adam was formed first, then Eve; and Adam was not deceived, but the woman was deceived and became a transgressor" (1 Tim. 2:9-14).

Here the apostle speaks particularly to a woman in relation to her husband, to be in subjection to him, and not to teach nor usurp authority over him. Therefore he mentions Adam and Eve. Let it be strained to the utmost, as the opposers of women's speaking would have it, that is, that they should not preach nor speak in the church, of which there is nothing here. The apostle is speaking to such as he is teaching to wear their apparel, what to wear and what not to wear—such as were not come to wear modest apparel, and such were not come to shamefacedness and sobriety. He was exhorting them from braided hair, gold, pearls, and costly array. Such are not to usurp authority over the man, but to learn in silence with all subjection, as it becomes women professing godliness with good works.

What is all this to such as have the power and Spirit of the Lord Jesus poured upon them, and have the message of the Lord Jesus given unto them? Must not they speak the word of the Lord, because of these indecent and irreverent women that the apostle speaks of, and to, in these two scriptures? How are the men of this generation blinded, that bring these scriptures and pervert the apostle's words and corrupt his intent in speaking of them? By these scriptures, [they] endeavor to stop the message and word of the Lord God in women, by con-demning and despising of them. If the apostle would have had women's speaking stopped and did not allow of them, why did he entreat his true yokefellow to help those women who la-bored with him in the gospel (Phil. 4:3)? Why did the apostles join together in prayer and supplication with the women, and Mary the mother of Jesus, and with his brethren (Acts 1:14), if they had not allowed and had union and fellowship with the Spirit of God, wherever it was revealed, in women as well as others? All this opposing, and gainsaying of women's speak-ing, has risen out of the bottomless pit and spirit of darkness that have spoken for these many hundred years together in this night of apostasy, since the revelations have ceased and been hid. That spirit has limited and bound all up within its bond and compass and so would suffer none to speak, but such as that spirit of darkness approved of, man or woman.

Here has been the misery of these last ages past, in the time of the reign of the beast, that John saw when he stood upon the sand of the sea, [the beast] rising out of the sea and out of the earth, having seven heads and ten horns (Rev. 13). In this [is seen the] great city of Babylon, which is the woman that has sat so long upon the scarlet colored beast, full of names of blasphemy, having seven heads and ten horns. This woman has been arrayed and decked with gold, pearls, and precious stones. She has had a golden cup in her hand, full of abomi-nations, and has made all nations drunk with the cup of her fornication. All the world has wandered after the beast and has worshiped the dragon that gave power to the beast. This woman has been drunk with the blood of the saints and with the blood of the martyrs of Jesus. This has been the woman that has been speaking and usurping authority for many hundred years together. Let the times and ages past testify how many have been murdered and slain, in ages and generations past, every religion and profession (as it has been called) killing and murdering one another, that would not join one with another. Thus the Spirit of Truth, and the power of the Lord Jesus Christ have been quite lost among them that have done this. This mother of harlots has sat as a queen and said she should see no sorrow. Her days have been long, even many hundreds of years—for there was power given unto the beast to continue forty and two months, to make war with the saints, and to overcome them—and all that have dwelt upon the earth have worshiped him whose names are not written in the book of the life of the Lamb, slain from the foundation of the world.

Blessed be the Lord, his time is over which was above twelve-hundred years. The darkness is past. The night of apostasy draws to an end and the true light now shines, the morning light, the bright morning star, the root and offspring of David. He is risen. He is risen, glory to the highest for evermore. The joy of the morning is come. The bride, the Lamb's wife, is making herself ready, as a bride that is adorning for her husband. To her is granted that she shall be arrayed in the fine linen, clean and white, and the fine linen is the righteousness of the saints. The holy Jerusalem is descending out of heaven from God, having the glory of God, and her light is like a jasper stone, clear as crystal.

This is that free woman, that all the children of the promise are born of—not the children of the bond-woman, which is Hagar, which genders to strife and to bondage, and which answers to Jerusalem, which is in bondage with her children. This is the Jerusalem which is free, which is the mother of us all. This bond-woman and her children, that are born after the flesh, have persecuted them that are born after the Spirit, even until now. Now the bond-woman and her seed are to be cast out, that have kept so long in bondage, in slavery, and under limits. This bond-woman and her brood are to be cast out. Our holy city, the new Jerusalem, is coming down from heaven. Her light will shine throughout the whole earth, even as a jasper-stone, clear as crystal, which brings freedom and liberty and perfect redemption to her whole seed. This is that woman and image of the eternal God that God has owned, does own, and will own for evermore.

More might be added to this purpose, both out of the Old Testament and New, where it is evident that God made no difference, but gave His good Spirit, as it pleased Him, both to man and woman, as Deborah, Huldah, and Sarah. The Lord calls by His prophet Isaiah, "Hearken to me, you who pursue deliverance, you who seek the Lord; look to the rock from which you were hewn, and to the quarry from which you were digged. Look to Abraham your father and to Sarah that bore you.... For the Lord will comfort Zion" (Isa. 51:1-3). Anna the prophetess, who was a widow of fourscore and four years of age, who departed not from the temple, but served God with fasting and prayers night and day: she, coming in at that instant (when old Simeon took the child Jesus in his arms), gave thanks unto the Lord, and spoke of Him to all them who looked for redemption in Jerusalem (Luke 2:36-38). Philip the Evangelist, who was one of the seven, into whose house the apostle Paul entered (Acts 6:1-6), had four daughters who were virgins, who did prophesy (Acts 21:8-9).

Let this serve to stop that opposing spirit that would limit the power and Spirit of the Lord Jesus, whose Spirit is poured upon all flesh, both sons and daughters, now in His resurrection—since that the Lord God in the creation, when He made man in His own image, He made them male and female; and since that Christ Jesus, as the apostle says, was made of a woman, the power of the highest overshadowed her, the Holy Ghost came upon her, and the holy Thing that was born of her was called the Son of God. When He was upon the earth, He manifested His love, His will, and His mind, both to the woman of Samaria, and Martha and Mary her sister, and several others, as has been showed. After His resurrection also, [He] manifested Himself unto them first of all, even before He ascended unto His Father. Now, when Jesus was risen, the first day of the week, He appeared first unto Mary Magdalene (Mark 16:9). Thus the Lord Jesus has manifested Himself and His power, without respect of persons. So let all mouths be stopped that would limit Him, whose power and Spirit are infinite, who is pouring it upon all flesh.

Thus much [is] in answer to these two scriptures which have been made such a stumbling block, which the ministers of darkness have made such a mountain of. The Lord is removing all this and taking it out of the way.

Margaret Fell

A Further Addition in Answer to the Objection
Concerning Women Keeping Silent in the Church:

"For they are not permitted to speak, but should be subordinate, as even the law says. If there is anything they desire to know, let them ask their husbands at home. For it is shameful for a woman to speak in church." Now this, as Paul writes in 1 Corinthians 14:34-35, is one with that of 1 Timothy 2:11: "Let a woman learn in silence with all submissiveness."

To which I say, if you tie this to all outward women, then there were many women that were widows, who had no husbands. Many were virgins, who had no husbands. Philip had four daughters that were prophetesses. Such would be despised, who the apostle did not forbid. If it were to all women, that no women might speak, then Paul would have contradicted himself, but they were such women that the apostle mentions in Timothy, that grew wanton, were busy-bodies, tattlers, and kicked against Christ. Christ in the male and in the female is one. He is the husband and His wife is the church. God has said that His daughters should prophesy as well as His sons. Where He has poured forth His Spirit upon them, they must prophesy, though blind priests say to the contrary and will not permit holy women to speak.

It is said, "they are not permitted to speak, but should be subordinate, as even the law says," but where women are led by the Spirit of God, they are not under the law, for Christ in the male and the female is one. Where He is made manifest in male and female, He may speak, for He is the end of the law for righteousness to all them that believe.

So here you ought to make a distinction what sort of women are forbidden to speak: such as were under the law, who were not come to Christ nor to the Spirit of prophecy. Huldah,

Miriam, and Hannah were prophetesses, who were not forbidden in the time of the law, for they all prophesied in the time of the law. You may read in 2 Kings 22:14f what Huldah said unto the priest and to the ambassadors that were sent to her from the king. She said, "Thus says the Lord, the God of Israel: Tell the man who sent you to me, 'Thus says the Lord, Behold, I will bring evil upon this place and upon its inhabitants, all the words of the book which the king of Judah has read.' Because they have forsaken me and have burned incense to other gods, that they might provoke me to anger with all the work of their hands, therefore my wrath will be kindled against this place, and it will not be quenched. But as to the king of Judah who sent you to inquire of the Lord, thus shall you say to him, 'Thus says the Lord, the God of Israel: Regarding the words which you have heard, because your heart was penitent, and you humbled yourself before the Lord, when you heard how I spoke against this place, and against its inhabitants, that they should become a desolation and a curse, and you have rent your clothes and wept before me, I also have heard you, says the Lord. Therefore, behold, I will gather you to your fathers, and you shall be gathered to your grave in peace, and your eyes shall not see all the evil which I will bring upon this place.'"

Now let us see if any of you, blind priests, can speak after this manner. See if it be not a better sermon than any of you can make, who are against women's speaking. Isaiah, who went to the prophetess, did not forbid her speaking or prophesying (8:3). Was it not prophesied in Joel 2:28f [KJV] that handmaids should prophesy? Are not handmaids women? Consider this, you that are against women's speaking, how in the Acts the Spirit of the Lord was poured forth upon daughters as well as sons. In the time of the gospel, when Mary came to salute Elizabeth in the hill country in Judea, when Elizabeth heard the salutation of Mary, the babe leaped in her womb and she was filled with the Holy Spirit. Elizabeth spoke with a loud voice, "'Blessed are you among women, and blessed is the fruit of your womb! And why is this granted me, that the mother of my Lord should come to me? For behold, when the voice of your greeting came to my ears, the babe in my womb leaped for joy. And blessed is she who believed that there would be a fulfillment of what was spoken to her from the Lord.' And Mary said, 'My soul magnifies the Lord, and my spirit rejoices in God my Savior, for He has regarded the low estate of His handmaiden. For behold, henceforth all generations will call me blessed; for He who is mighty has done great things for me, and holy is His name. And His mercy is on those who fear Him from generation to generation. He has shown strength with His arm, He has scattered the proud in the imagination of their hearts, He has put down the mighty from their thrones, and exalted those of low degree; He has filled the hungry with good things, and the rich He has sent empty away. He has helped His servant Israel, in remembrance of His mercy, as He spoke to our fathers, to Abraham, and to his posterity forever'" (Luke 1:42-55). Are you not here beholding to the woman for her sermon, to use her words to put into your [Book of] Common Prayer? Yet you forbid women's speaking.

Here you may see how these two women prophesied of Christ and preached better than all the blind priests did in that age, better than this age also who are beholding to women to make use of their words. See in the book of Ruth (4:10f), how the women blessed her in the gate of the city, of whose stock came Christ: "May the Lord make the woman, who is coming into your house, like Rachel and Leah, who together built up the house of Israel. May you prosper in Ephrathah and be renowned in Bethlehem; and may your house be like the house of

Perez, whom Tamar bore to Judah, because of the children that the Lord will give you by this young woman…. Blessed be the Lord, who has not left you this day without next of kin; and may His name be renowned in Israel!" Also see in the first chapter of Samuel, how Hannah prayed and spoke in the temple of the Lord, "O Lord of hosts, if thou wilt indeed look on the affliction of thy maidservant, and remember me, and not forget thy maidservant" (1 Sam. 1:11). Read in the second chapter of Samuel, how she rejoiced in God, and said, "My heart exults in the Lord; my strength is exalted in the Lord. My mouth derides my enemies, because I rejoice in thy salvation. There is none holy like the Lord, there is none besides thee; there is no rock like our God. Talk no more so very proudly, let not arrogance come from your mouth; for the Lord is a God of knowledge, and by Him actions are weighed. The bows of the mighty are broken, but the feeble gird on strength. Those who were full have hired themselves out for bread, but those who were hungry have ceased to hunger. The barren has borne seven, but she who has many children is forlorn. The Lord kills and brings to life; He brings down to sheol and raises up. The Lord makes poor and makes rich; He brings low, He also exalts. He raises up the poor from the dust; He lifts the needy from the ash heap, to make them sit with princes and inherit a seat of honor. For the pillars of the earth are the Lord's, and on them He has set the world. He will guard the feet of His faithful ones; but the wicked shall be cut off in darkness; for not by might shall a man prevail. The adversaries of the Lord shall be broken to pieces; against them He will thunder in heaven. The Lord will judge the ends of the earth; He will give strength to His king, and exalt the power of His anointed" (1 Samuel 2:1-10).

Thus you may see what a woman has said, when old Eli the priest thought she had been drunk. See if any of you blind priests, that speak against women's speaking, can preach after this manner, who cannot make such a sermon as this woman did, and yet will make a trade of this woman's and other women's words.

Did not the Queen of Sheba speak, that came to Solomon, received the law of God, preached it in her kingdom, blessed the Lord God that loved Solomon and set him on the throne of Israel, because the Lord loved Israel for ever, and made the king to do equity and righteousness? This was the language of the Queen of Sheba (see 1 Kings 10).

See what glorious expressions Queen Esther used to comfort the people of God who were the church of God (as you may read in the book of Esther). [She] caused joy and gladness of heart among all the Jews who prayed and worshiped the Lord in all places, who jeoparded her life contrary to the King's command, went and spoke to the King in the wisdom and fear of the Lord by which means she saved the lives of the people of God. Righteous Mordecai did not forbid her speaking, but said if she held her peace, she and her father's house should be destroyed. Here in you blind priests are contrary to righteous Mordecai.

Likewise you may read how Judith spoke, what noble acts she did, how she spoke to the elders of Israel, and said, "Now therefore, brethren, let us set an example to our brethren.... In spite of everything let us give thanks to the Lord our God, who is putting us to the test as he did our forefathers. Remember what He did with Abraham, and how He tested Isaac, and what happened to Jacob in Mesopotamia in Syria, while he was keeping the sheep of Laban, his mother's brother. For he has not tried us with fire, as He did them, to search their hearts..." (The New Oxford Annotated Bible with the Apocrypha, Judith 8:24-27). Read also her prayer in the Book of Judith and how the elders commended her and said, "All that you have said has been spoken out of a true heart, and there is no one who can deny your words…. So pray for us, since you are a devout woman…" (Judith 8:28, 31). So these elders of Israel did not forbid her speaking, as you blind priests do. Yet you will make a trade of women's words to get money by, take texts and preach sermons upon women's words. And still cry out, women must not speak, women must be silent. So you are far from the minds of the elders of Israel, who praised God for a woman's speaking. The Jezebel, and the woman, the false church, the great whore, and tattling and unlearned women and busy-bodies, which have a long time spoke and tattled, are forbidden to preach. [They] are forbidden to speak by the true church which Christ is the head of—such women as were in transgression under the law, which are called "a woman" in the Revelations.

See further how the wise woman cried to Joab over the wall and saved the city of Abel as you may read (2 Sam. 20:16f), how in her wisdom she spoke to Joab, saying, "I am one of those who are peaceable and faithful in Israel; you seek to destroy a city which is a mother in Israel; why will you swallow up the heritage of the Lord?" Then went the woman to the people in her wisdom, and smote off the head of Sheba, that rose up against David, the Lord's anointed. Then Joab blew the trumpet and all the people departed in peace. This deliverance was by the means of a woman's speaking, but tattlers and busy-bodies are forbidden to preach by the true woman, [to] whom Christ is the husband—to the woman as well as the man, all being comprehended to be the church. In this true church, sons and daughters do prophesy.

Women labor in the gospel. But the apostle permits not tattlers, busy-bodies, and such as usurp authority over the man, who would not have Christ to reign nor speak, neither in the male nor female. Such the law permits not to speak. Such must learn of their husbands. But what husbands have widows to learn of, but Christ? Was not Christ the husband of Philip's four daughters? May not they that are learned of their husbands speak then? But Jezebel, and tattlers, and the whore, that deny revelation and prophecy, are not permitted, who will not learn of Christ? They that are out of the Spirit and power of Christ that the prophets were in, [they] who are in the transgression, are ignorant of the scriptures. Such are against women's speaking, and men's too, who preach that which they have received of the Lord God. That which they have preached and do preach will come over all your heads, yea, over the head of the false church, the Pope. The false church is the Pope's wife. So he and they that be of him, and come from him are against women's speaking in the true church (when both he and the false church are called "woman," in Rev. 17) and so are in the transgression that would usurp authority over the man Christ Jesus and His wife too, and would not have Him to reign. But the judgment of the great whore is come.

Christ is the head of the church, the true woman, which is His wife. In it do daughters prophesy, who are above the Pope and his wife, and atop of them. Here Christ is the head of the male and female who may speak. The church is called a royal priesthood; so the woman must offer as well as the man. Revelation 22:17 [says]: "The Spirit and the Bride say, 'Come.'" So is not the bride the church? Does the church only consist of men? You that deny women's speaking, answer [this]: does it not consist of women, as well as men? Is not the bride compared to the whole church? Does not the bride say, "Come"? Does not the woman speak then, the husband, Christ Jesus, the Amen? Does not the false church go about to stop the bride's mouth? But it is not possible, for the bridegroom is with His bride. He opens her mouth. Christ Jesus—who goes on conquering, and to conquer, who kills and slays with the sword which is the word of His mouth—the Lamb and the saints shall have the victory, the true speakers of men and women over the false speaker.

Margaret Fell

CHAPTER 4

SOME RANTERS' PRINCIPLES ANSWERED

Historical Introduction

Margaret Fell's little pamphlet, *Some Ranters' Principles Answered*, is one of her most vehement. In fact, persons who carry the mistaken stereotype of early Quakers as meek, nonmilitant, retiring individuals will be shocked by the vigor of her denunciations ("blasphemy," "You dark blind sot," "abominable are you") and her pronouncements of damnation. Fell's general writing style is always plain, straight forward, and frank, but here the natural vigor is accentuated by the need to distinguish with pristine clearness the Quaker position from that of the Ranters and to leave no doubt in her readers' minds as to the utter Quaker rejection of the Ranters. The reasons for the forcefulness of Fell's response lies in the nature of Ranterism and the problems and dangers it created for Quakers.

Who were the Ranters? They were a very loose movement which appeared during the civil unrest, intellectual ferment, and political chaos of Commonwealth England in the 1640s, about the same period George Fox began his ministry. Their name comes from the extravagant manner in which they often proclaimed their views.

Those views were essentially antinomian, a term coming from two Greek words meaning "against law." J. MacBride Sterrett's article on the subject in *The Encyclopedia of Religion and Ethics* notes that early Reformation antinomianism "directed itself towards the destruction of the Moral Law of the Old Testament in the interest of the new freedom of Christians and the Testimony of the Spirit" (582). At first glance, the early Quaker proclamation, "that Christ had come to teach His people today," and the Quaker belief that as a people they were to be directed by His Spirit, being brought off obedience to the Mosaic Law and into obedience with the will of God, would seem to be antinomian. That, indeed, is where public confusion over the difference between Ranters and Quakers began. This is also where the similarity between the two positions ended, for the Quakers with their firm grounding in prophetic Christianity and the foundation of prophetic righteousness did not fall into the ethical anarchism of the Ranters.

The very subjectivity and individualism of the Ranter position prevented it from either becoming a sect or developing a vision of order and community. It led, instead, to a marked rejection of values, values necessary for the development of community. As Sterrett observes, "In its widest sense the term [antinomianism] is used to designate the doctrines of extreme fanatics who deny subjection to any law other than the subjective caprices of the empirical individual, though this individual is generally credited as the witness and interpreter of the Holy Spirit" (582).

Clearly, the position Margaret Fell addresses in *Some Ranters' Principles Answered* fits this description. The unidentified writer and pamphlet she quotes clearly expresses its theological assumptions: "God is darkness as well as light, and there is but one power." Thus, "nothing is contrary to the one power which is God.... Whatever is done, it is His will." The moral relativism of this position is quickly made plain when Margaret's opponent asserts, "Man, in his carnal apprehensions of God, calls one thing good and another thing evil, but in Him all things are good, for all things are of Him." "Whatsoever has been done in darkness may be done in the light, as swearing, lying, drunkenness, cheating—which being done in the light, are done in faith, and what is of faith is not sin."

The logical simplicity of the Ranter position made it attractive to many during the rampant questioning of old religious, social, and political values which marked the Commonwealth period between 1644 and 1660. During this period, the Ranters made enough headway that Parliament enacted strong legislation against them and at least one government official expressed the view, but for the Quakers, Ranterism would have swept England. While that assessment may overstate the case, there is an element of truth in it.

Most of the clergy—be they conformist or nonconformist—were no match for either the Quakers or the Ranters. The clergy, holding their positions usually through family or political connections, were ill-trained in theological disputation, poorly read in scripture, and ungrounded in serious religious faith. A man of George Fox's depth, whose life swam in scripture and whose understanding was illuminated by the Holy Spirit, became a terror to the average priests and preachers in his time, overturning their feeble arguments and exposing their misquotes and misappropriations of scripture. To the Quaker query as to whether the clergy "spoke from that Spirit which was in Christ, the prophets, and the apostles," the priests and preachers could only utter a cowed negative.

While the Ranters were forward and extravagant in their claims to spiritual insight, their arguments were as feebly and inappropriately grounded in scripture as the clergy's. In fact, Margaret Fell's opponent is bested and overturned in his scriptural proofs by her own superior knowledge of the Bible quite as smartly and decisively as were many of Fox's opponents by his.

The Quaker need to confront Ranterism was concrete and imperative. Fox and other traveling ministers found it often turning up unexpectedly. For instance, in 1649, Fox visited the prison in Coventry having heard of a people imprisoned for religion. However, the people he found were Ranters who "began to rant and vapour and blaspheme" (*Journal*, 46-47). At other moments, they could be rude and annoying. In Leicestershire in 1655, we find them singing, whistling, and dancing derogatorily before Fox (*Journal*, 182-183).

In fact, the nature of Quaker worship, a silent waiting on the Spirit, made Quaker gatherings seemingly an easy target for Ranter disruption. The Ranters, with their wild imaginings and lack of spiritual seriousness—let alone commonsense decorum—often proved an initial cross for Quaker Meetings to carry. Yet, though the Ranters rose to jangle and jar the new worship, an able Spirit-led Quaker ministry proved equal to the challenge as it confronted and at times reached the discordant souls it addressed.

Thus, while these Ranter tactics proved an annoyance, they were not so serious as the often enunciated Ranter claim that there was no difference between Ranters and Quakers that the latter would "grow up" into Ranterism—a claim that Fell's opponent makes. The anger and horror with which she greets this claim can only fully be comprehended by understanding the background from which they sprang: the utter repugnance she feels over their degraded lives, the essential doctrinal differences of Quakerism, the danger inherent in identification with the Ranters, and the sufferings caused by Ranters through the misunderstanding and misidentification they fostered.

Content Introduction

First, Fell's repugnance at the immorality of the Ranters saturates her response to them. In the Ranters, we have more than a mere intellectual difference of opinion. The Ranters lived their antinomianism and the long list of wrongs they often openly confessed to, and reveled in, commonly included lying, cheating, whoring, adultery, and drunkenness. Suspicion of plottings, murder, and treason were sometimes well grounded. The Ranter amorality that fronted as religion made its practitioners not only untrustworthy, but inherently destructive of community. They were often disgusting, sometimes dangerous, and always suspect.

Beyond Fell's disgust lies her clear perception that the doctrinal differences between Ranters and Quakers are absolutely irreconcilable and in deadly conflict with one another. While both groups witnessed the passing of the Mosaic Law and its hold over those who entered into liberty of the sons and daughters of God, the prophetic Christianity of the first Quakers led straightway to conclusions opposite those of the Ranters. Clearly, the whole of redemptive history is that of God seeking righteousness from His people. God is a God of light in whom there is no darkness, a God who seeks His people, who demands lightness of them, and who gives them the power to obey Him. In place of the outward direction of the Mosaic Law, the new covenant witnesses the presence of Christ Jesus perfecting the law of God.

While on first consideration there appears to be potential here for the same subjective individualism rampant among Ranters, early Quakers saw two checks against such danger: the scriptural witness and the faithful community. Quakers viewed the work of God in Christ and in the prophets and apostles as spiritually definitive, as an important measure against which they could judge truly whether they were in that Spirit and Life the apostles and prophets were in.

Just as they challenged the Christendom of their day with the declaration that it did not reflect the embodiment of Christ and His teaching, so they knew they would be so measured. In fact, the new creation in Christ—the new person—is clearly defined in the declarations of the apostles (like Col. 3:5-13) and these were often held up by Friends and Margaret Fell as the outward evidence that the Spirit was within.

Beyond scripture, there was the second check: the faithful community. Obviously, fallen human nature contains great rationalizing abilities and remarkable skills in self-foolery. Early Quakers were well aware of this. Over against this, they believed in the logical consistency of the will of God: that He does not will, or declare against an action in one person, only to demand the opposite behavior in another. Thus, if those who sought and waited upon the will of God found unity in the Spirit concerning some action and that unity was not contradicted by the witness of scripture, then one was proceeding rightly. However, if the opposite was true, stiff soul-searching was in order.

Beyond morals and doctrine, there were particular dangers in being identified with Ranter anarchism and Quakers suffered dearly when the Commonwealth confused the positions of the two groups. There is no better witness to this than the fallout on the Quaker movement from the Nayler Affair. James Nayler—one of the most brilliant, remarkable, and charismatic of the early Quaker preachers, a rival to Fox in success and stature—fell increasingly under the influence of certain Ranters who were gathering in the wake of this work, particularly Martha Simmonds, who was being especially influential in her extravagant regard for and praise of Nayler. Usually sharp sighted, Nayler himself was debilitated by the exhausting work of travel, ministry, and harsh fasting. In the last days of October, 1656, he allowed his followers to lead him into Bristol on horseback in imitation of the entry of Jesus into Jerusalem. In his pockets

were letters from Thomas Simmonds, Martha's husband, addressing him as "Thou King of Israel and son of the Most high." Arrest
for blasphemy was immediate and the evidence seemed damning!
Nayler was tried by the last Parliament of Cromwell's Commonwealth. Whether Nayler's entrance to Bristol was merely the prophetic re-enactment of a sign, whether he was perhaps framed and
railroaded, are beside the point. The clear line between the Everlasting Gospel declared by the Quakers and the radical anarchism of the
Ranters had been confused, breached, and momentarily obscured.

Quakers suffered dearly for the Nayler Affair. Francis Howgill
wrote Fell that Nayler and his followers "made Truth stink" by their
actions. It was the pretext needed by the enemies of Quakerism to
turn government and society against the burgeoning movement.
Thousands of Friends were swept into jail, Meetings were broken up,
and widespread persecution occurred. The deaths, maimings, beatings, and distrainment of goods—the sufferings of those who continued to bear faithful witness to truth—and the difficulties met by
Quaker ministers continuing the work of declaring the Gospel were
so bitter that George Fox appears to have never found the openness
to be fully reconciled with Nayler when the latter turned penitent
and sought forgiveness. Against the backdrop of Ranter activities
and Nayler's debacle late in the autumn of 1656, the vehemence of
Some Ranters' Principles Answered is both understandable and necessary. The difference in principles between Friend and Ranter had to
be sharply and uncompromisingly defined.

Isabel Ross, in her notes to *Margaret Fell: Mother of Quakerism*,
observes that *Some Ranters' Principles Answered* was omitted from
Margaret Fell's works when they were published in 1710, eight years
after her death—"possibly because by that time Ranterism was no
longer a dangerous movement" (103). However, the present editor
has chosen to include it here, because, while Commonwealth Ranterism may have withered long ago, the antinomian spirit that was

its source is as old as Christianity and very much evident in twentieth century Christendom. We find the ancient apostles warning the church against twisted teachers and teachings that suggest that life in Christ gives excuse for amoral behaviors. Nietzsche's doctrine of the unvaluing of all values, the "Die Unwertung aller Werte," is a reflection of only one of many antinomian trends that have manifested themselves over the last one-hundred years. The Follow-Your-Nature-Against-The-Rules attitude, prevalent in twentieth century America and markedly present in Quakerism are only the latest examples of an old destructive, and today largely unchallenged, antinomianism.

Thus, it seems appropriate to include Margaret Fell's pamphlet here, for it defines true Christian liberty in the Everlasting Gospel with Christ as teacher who leads His sheep into rightness of behavior through His inward guidance. Set within the larger context of her writings and the declaration of the Everlasting Gospel,[1] *Some Answers to Ranters' Principles* makes it clear that early Quakers grasped the revolutionary mystery of the new creation, the new person whose heart is recreated through the power of God, to manifest the true fruits of rightness—love, kindness, gentleness, compassion. Perhaps works without faith could not win redemption, but clearly the ground and foundation of a faith that produced no good works was to be just as suspect.

Some Ranters' Principles Answered

A Testimony Of The Touchstone For All Professions, And All Forms, And Gathered Churches (As They Call Them) Of What Sort Soever To Try Their Ground And Foundation By,

And

A Trial By The Scriptures, [Of] Who The False Prophets Are, Who Are In The World, Who John Said Should Be In The Last Times

By
Margaret Fell

Also

Some Ranters' Principles Answered

"Therefore thus says the Lord God, 'Behold, I am laying in Zion for a foundation a stone, a tested stone, a precious cornerstone, of a sure foundation'" (Isa. 28:16).

"The stone which the builders rejected has become the chief cornerstone" (Ps. 118:22).

"So then you are no longer strangers and sojourners, but you are
fellow citizens with the saints and members of the household
of God, built upon the foundation of the apostles and prophets,
Christ Jesus himself being the chief cornerstone..." (Eph. 2:19-20).

"To you therefore who believe, He is precious, but for those who do
not believe, 'The very stone which the builders rejected has become
the head of the corner'..." (1 Pet. 2:7).

London

Printed for Thomas Simmons, at the sign of the Bull and Mouth
near Aldersgate 1656.

An Answer to the Ranters' Principles

The word of the Lord to you Ranters everywhere, where this may come, who are of the generation whose hearts are turned away from the Lord God and serve the gods of the nations: Your root bears gall and wormwood. You are under the curse and your blessings are cursed, though you may bless yourselves in your hearts saying: "I shall have peace, though I walk in the imagination of mine heart, to add drunkenness to thirst." The Lord will not spare you when His anger kindles and His jealousy smokes. Then all the curses that are written in the book shall lie upon you and your name shall be blotted out from under heaven (quote and paraphrase from Deut. 29:19-20 KJV).

RANTERS: God is darkness as well as light, and there is but one power, etc.

ANSWER: That is blasphemy. Your message is for the prince of darkness. You are in the land of darkness, and the shadow of death, where your light is darkness, where you are driven from the light into darkness, under the curse, under the power of the prince of the air who rules the children of disobedience, separated from God. There you shall have your portion. He who is the messenger of the living God, who declares that which was from the beginning, which He had heard, which He had seen and handled (the Word of life), which bears witness unto the living God: this is the message that He declares: "That God is light and in Him is no darkness at all" (1 John 1:5). You that say this knows not Him who is the covenant of light, who is given a light to enlighten the Gentiles, but [you] are one that does evil and hates the light, neither comes to the light, lest your deeds should be reproved. Therefore you are for condemnation with the light. The apostle says, "What fellowship has light with darkness?" (2 Cor. 6:14). You say, God is darkness as well as light. You say there is but one power, but you shall find another power then: that which you act under and for and in, [that] which shall overturn and confound you and your power and turn you into the bottomless pit, [that] which is the beast which has seven heads and ten horns. Upon your head are the names of blasphemy. You worship the dragon and give your power unto the beast. You speak great things and blasphemies, but your power is limited (see Rev. 13:1-7). You bring two scriptures, Colossians 3:11 and Ephesians 1:11, which neither of them belongs to you, nor none of your generation, who are enemies of God and all righteousness.

RANTERS: Nothing is contrary to the one power, which is God; nothing works against Him; nothing opposes Him; nothing is contrary to His will. Whatever is done, it is His will.

ANSWER: That is likewise false and blasphemy. You and your power are contrary and act contrary to the power of God. Therefore do you and your power give life unto the image of the beast, that the image of the beast should speak and does speak in you. You worship the dragon, which gives power unto the beast (Rev. 13:1-7, 15), and you exercise the power of the first beast, whose deadly wound was healed. This, your power, is contrary to the power of God. The power of the living God shall bind and chain you and the dragon whom you worship, and shall cast you into the pit. You, nor none in your nature, nor of your spirit nor power, does the will of God, for he that does the will of God enters into the kingdom, which you nor none of your generation ever shall. He that does the will of God is He whom God has sent, of whom it is written in the volume of the book: "Lo, I come to do your will, O God." It is His meat and drink to do the will of Him that sent Him, which you know nothing of, but are an enemy to Him and all who are of Him and act in your filthy will, which is of the flesh, lust, and uncleanness, wallowing in your filthiness. You are shut out from God and all who are of him, for by the will of God, we are sanctified through the offering of the body of Jesus Christ once for all, which you are an enemy to, and are shut from forever.

RANTERS: Man, in his carnal apprehensions of God, calls one thing good and another thing evil, but in Him all things are good, for all things are of Him.

ANSWER: You dark blind sot. You are in your carnal apprehensions and so neither know the good nor the evil, but are under the woe and are him which calls evil good and good evil, [which] puts darkness for light and light for darkness, [which] puts bitter for sweet and sweet for bitter (Isa. 5:18-23). You enemy of the living God, [you] know not what is in Him, neither are you of Him, but are in your sins and filthiness, separated from Him and all who are of Him. You bring a scripture in 2 Corinthians 5:18 which is nothing to you, who are in your filthiness and uncleanness, for who the apostle spoke to there: it was the new creature, where the old things were passed away and all things were become new. You are in your old sins and old filthiness yet. Christ Jesus, who is the reconciliation of all things that are of God, is your condemnation and shall be your destruction forever.

RANTERS: While man calls one thing good, and another thing evil, he sees not with the eye of God, who saw all things very good.

ANSWER: You are blind from your birth, you do not see with the eye of God, and therefore do not know the good nor the evil. Who sees with the eye of God sees you to be evil and that seed which causes the evil and brought the curse upon the earth for your sake and the creature under the bondage of corruption, who goes upon your belly, and dust do you eat. The eye of God turns you, the wicked and all that forget God, into hell, which is your place of torment which you shall find. To you, nothing is good.

RANTERS: All things are reconciled to the one power which is God: earth and heaven, light and darkness, good and evil.

ANSWER: You who are for torments and flames would be reconciled to God, but you shall find the wrath of the Lamb, who is come to torment you before your time (Matt. 8:29f).[1] Weeping and wailing you shall find (Mark 5:7; Luke 8:28).[2] There is no reconciliation to God for you, who are drunk with the wine of the wrath of her[3] fornication, worship the beast and his image, and receive his mark in your forehead. Therefore shall you drink of the wine of the wrath of God, which is poured out without mixture into the cup of His indignation, and shall be tormented with fire and brimstone in the presence of His holy angels and in the presence of the Lamb (Rev. 14:8-10). This you shall eternally witness, who would have light and darkness reconciled together. You bring a scripture in 2 Corinthians 5:19: To wit, that God is in Christ reconciling the world unto Himself. But to Christ Jesus, by which all things are reconciled, you are an enemy of Him, of His truth, and of all righteousness. If light and darkness had been one, as you say, Christ needed not have come to reconcile the world to Himself, so you have brought this scripture to your own destruction to make your blasphemy more manifest.[4]

RANTERS: That which is evil to one is good to another. One man's light is another's darkness. One man accounts it sin to observe a day. Another accounts it sin not to observe a day. The third is free to both, either to observe or not to observe, for he is brought into the liberty of the sons of God and is free to all things.

ANSWER: That which is good to you is evil to all who are of God. Abominable are you and that which you live in, to God and all who are obedient to His will. The light that is in you is darkness. How great is that darkness! You are in [the] bondage and slavery of sin, your filthy lusts and uncleanness, and servant to them. So you are not so much as observing a day, or not a day, unto the Lord. [You] are the servant of sin and uncleanness, speaking great swelling words of vanity and alluring through the lusts of the flesh through much wantonness those who were clean escaped from you who live in error. So while you are promising yourselves liberty, you, yourselves, are the servants of corruption (2 Pet. 2:18-19). Of whom a man is overcome, of the same he is brought into bondage. The liberty of the sons of God [neither] you nor none of your spirit shall ever know. You who have liberties to all things are shut out from the liberty of the sons of God, which is purchased by the Son of God who binds and chains you and your liberty.

RANTERS: Man, in his carnal apprehensions of the one power which is God, calls one thing clean and another thing unclean, but in the sight of God all things are good and clean. To man that esteems and apprehends a thing to be evil, to him it is evil, but in the sight of God, all things and all ways are clean and good.

ANSWER: You who are carnal and in your apprehensions know not the power which is of God, nor favor the things which be of God, and that which puts the difference between the clean and unclean and makes the separation between the precious and the vile—to this you are an enemy. This has found you out and has separated you and all of your spirit from God and all who are of Him. On the left hand among the goats, you are. All of your nature and of your spirit are for the fire and destruction. The sword of the Lord shall cut you down, root and branch, who are the cursed tree, that cannot bring forth good fruit. In the sight of God, you are filthy, polluted, unclean, who to you is a consuming fire. You are before Him as stubble. You bring a scripture in Romans 14:14, where the apostle says, there is "nothing unclean of itself." To you who are unclean, filthy and polluted, there is nothing clean. All is defiled by you, who live in the lust of uncleanness.

RANTERS: Whatsoever has been done in darkness may be done in the light, as swearing, lying, drunkenness, cheating—which being done in the light, are done in faith, and what is of faith is not sin.

ANSWER: Here you have made it manifest that your light is darkness, that your faith is vain who are yet in your sins, that your God is the god of the world, that the devil who is the father of lies and of oaths and drunkenness and of all sin is your god.[5] So, as I said to you before, you and your god are to be bound and chained by the angel who has the key of the bottomless pit, are to be cast into the lake of fire and brimstone where the beast and the false prophets are, and shall be tormented day and night for ever (Rev. 20:10).

RANTERS: One power acts all things, which appear sometimes in darkness and sometimes in light, sometimes in glory, sometimes in shame as to the creature. Yet, in God, light and darkness, glory and shame are one. I, the Lord, do all these things—so one power.

ANSWER: That power that acts [in] you is limited, bound, chained, and comprehended. Your compass is known and seen with that which was before you and your power were, which seals you up in your torment for evermore. Your glory is your shame. Your God is your belly, who minds earthly things. Your power acts in the darkness. With the Light which never changes, which comes from Jesus who is the light of the world, you are condemned into the pit of darkness. From God who is the Father of light, who does all things by His power, you are shut eternally.

RANTERS: All things that be are brought out by one wisdom; which inventions all that are found out by one wisdom are found out.[6] No invention opposes this wisdom, every invention being found out by this wisdom.

ANSWER: Here, you serpent, are [you] spewing forth your poison and blasphemy, indeed, which would lay the deceit and subtlety of the serpent, which lodges in your bosom, upon God. But the Lord God lifts up His hand against you, to overthrow your seed, who has joined yourself to Baal-Peor and provoked the Lord to anger with your inventions. The plagues shall break in upon you, for the Lord will take vengeance upon your inventions, who are defiled with your own works and go whoring after your own inventions (Ps. 99:8; Ps. 106; Ps. 28:3-5). The righteous God will be avenged on you for your blasphemy. You bring a scripture in Proverbs 8:12, where Solomon says, "I wisdom dwell with prudence, and find out knowledge of witty inventions" [KJV].[7] Oh, you blasphemous beast! This is a mystery to you who live in your lusts and uncleanness. He says in the next verse: "The fear of the Lord is hatred of evil. Pride and arrogance and the way of evil and perverted speech I hate." Do you so, who are pleading for all manner of vileness and filthiness? O you abominable wretch, who live in that which Solomon hated.

RANTERS: Men, in their dark knowledge of the one power in his several workings, say one number worships one God, the god of the world, another company a God which is not of the world, whereas God is but one, working according to the good pleasure of His will.

ANSWER: You who are in dark knowledge, under the prince of the power of darkness, do not know nor ever shall know the eternal power of the living God, but to your destruction, for He is come and made manifest, who reproves the world of sin, of righteousness, and of judgment (John 16:8).[8] Now is the time that you and your God are judged, and your number, as you call them, who are of the number of the beast (Rev. 13:18).[9] The one God, which was before you and your god was, you know not, which shall be God when you are in the lake [of fire].

RANTERS: God loves and takes pleasure in all things in darkness as well as in the light, for darkness and light are both alike to Him.

ANSWER: That is false and blasphemy, for in you, who are darkness, God does not take pleasure, neither love. "For thou art not a God who delights in wickedness; evil may not sojourn with thee. The boastful may not stand before thy eyes; thou hatest all evil doers. Thou destroyest those who speak lies; the Lord abhors bloodthirsty and deceitful men" (Ps. 5:4-6). "Oh, that there were one among you who would shut the doors, that you might not kindle fire upon my altar in vain! I have no pleasure in you, says the Lord of hosts, and I will not accept an offering from your hand" (Mal. 1:10). You bring a scripture in Psalm 139:12, which scripture you shall witness fulfilled upon you, for your darkness shall not hide you nor cover you. The Almighty shall find you out: and the wrath of the Lamb. You who do live in pleasures on the earth, are wanton, and nourish your heart as in a day of slaughter, and have condemned and killed the just (James 5:5), you shall receive the reward of unrighteousness as they that count it pleasure to riot in the day time (2 Pet. 2:13), who are lovers of pleasure more than lovers of God and are serving diverse lusts and pleasures (2 Tim. 3:4; Titus 3:3).[10]

RANTERS: One power does all things, evil and good (being so to the low apprehensions of man, but all alike in God).

ANSWER: That is false and blasphemy. That power that acts [in] you does evil and cannot be good. You are the evil and not the good, [you] who call the evil good and the good evil. You are he that hates the good and loves the evil (Rom. 3:12; Mic. 3:2). Your resurrection shall be for damnation (John 5:29). You bring a scripture, Amos 3:6, which is fulfilling.[11] The Lion is roaring. The prey is taken. The bird is fallen into the snare, the trumpet is blowing in the city, and you are afraid. The evil that shall be done unto you, the Lord does it.

RANTERS: Darkness may be made light, as the one power makes Himself known, who is light, and all whose deeds are light, though darkness to the creatures' present apprehension.

ANSWER: You, who are darkness itself, and so an enemy to the light and a hater of the light, you shall never see light. To you, the eternal power of the living God is made known for your destruction. Where Christ is made manifest, He is made manifest to destroy the works of the devil. You are vain in your imaginations and your foolish heart is darkened.

RANTERS: I bring a scripture, Isaiah 42:16, where it is said, "And I will lead the blind in a way that they know not, in paths that they have not known I will guide them. I will turn the darkness before them into light, the rough places into level ground."

ANSWER: Here let the scripture confound you,[12] who are yet blind and unled into the way. The paths that you are in lead to destruction. The way of peace you know not, but are in the crooked ways of filthiness and uncleanness and are not yet come to be ashamed of your graven images and molten images which you call your gods.

RANTERS: What does holiness save, or ungodliness destroy, as you apprehend them to be?

ANSWER: Holiness saves that which you, the ungodly, destroy. The Lord God, who is a jealous God, His anger is kindled against you and will destroy you from the face of the earth. He that defiles the temple of God, him will God destroy, and miserably will He destroy the wicked men (Matt. 21:41).[13] You that make the members of Christ the members of a harlot and say meat is for the belly and the belly for meat: God shall destroy both it and you. The body is not for fornication, but for the Lord (1 Cor. 6:13, 15). Now we know what has [been] withheld that He might be revealed in His time. The mystery of iniquity does already work in you. Only he who lets will let, until he be taken out of the way. Then shall that wicked [one] be revealed whom the Lord shall consume with the spirit of His mouth and shall destroy with the brightness of His coming, that they might all be damned who believe not the truth, but had pleasure in unrighteousness (2 Thes. 2:3-13). Here is your portion. This you shall find fulfilled and witnessed to your destruction, for you—son of perdition and man of sin—are revealed.

RANTERS: [I] bring a scripture in the 12th chapter of Ecclesiastes, verse 7, where it is said, "...dust returns to the earth as it was, and the spirit returns to God who gave it."

ANSWER: He that spoke this lived not in filthiness and uncleanness, for He says that which you live in is vanity, which you, filthy beast, would set up, which was pulled down in Him. Neither do you know those conditions He spoke before He said these words. To you, they are a mystery. Your spirit does not return to God, for to the place of torment among the devils and damned in hell does your spirit return, where is weeping, wailing, and gnashing of teeth.

RANTERS: That which befalls the sons of men befalls beasts. They have all one breath. All go to one place. As the one dies, so dies the other. All are of the dust and turn to the dust. What preeminence has a man above a beast?

ANSWER: You are as the beast that perishes, who are in the place of judgment where wickedness is, and the place of your righteousness where iniquity is, which is all in the wickedness and transgression. Now is the time that God is judging you. You are made manifest to be the beast and the false prophet which is to be turned into the lake. This befalls all the sons of men who are in the beastly nature you live in and all who are in that nature that worships the beast and go all into one place of torment, as you shall find. That which is prepared for the lake shall not return to the dust, though you would have it so, you beast—and your spirit which is of the beast, that goes downward to the earth. You know not the spirit of a man that goes upward. You are he whom the decree of the most high is gone forth against. Your portion is with the beasts of the field. You are driven from the sons of men. Your heart is made fat like the beast's. Your dwelling is with the wild asses (Dan. 5:21).[14]

RANTERS: Man in his carnal apprehensions of God accounts one thing lawful and another thing unlawful, calls one way godly and another way ungodly. When as, there is no such thing, for he that is in the liberty of the sons of God—to him all things are lawful as they were to Paul.

ANSWER: You, who are in your carnal apprehensions of God, are in the world without God. You are alive without the law, [have] not come to know the law yet, and are dead in sins and trespasses. You, that live in pleasure, are dead while you live. You live unto sin and so are free from righteousness. The law which is holy, just, and good, shall cut you to pieces. You are not yet come to know the law, nor what is lawful, which every one passes through before they come to know the liberty of the sons of God—which law cuts down all your carnal apprehensions of God. Oh, you blasphemer, do you say that there is no such thing as lawful and unlawful, godliness and ungodliness? Would you lay waste the scriptures and make void the righteous law of God which takes hold of the transgressor? Would you trample upon the blood of the new covenant and count it an unholy thing? Oh, the day of vengeance is coming upon you. The Lord God is clothed with vengeance against you and all such as you are.

You who sit at the table of devils are shut out from the liberty of the sons of God and know not the condition that Paul had passed through. When you know that, it will be death and destruction to you. This you shall eternally witness, before ever you come to know the living God.[15]

RANTERS: This is the liberty that the sons of God are to stand fast in and to thrust out that which would show any evil in anything whatsoever: seeing in God all things are lawful and for everything under the sun there is a time and a season.

ANSWER: You blasphemous beast that thrusts out all that would show any evil in anything, who are in your fleshly liberty, lust of uncleanness, and all manner of filthiness. You are shut out from the presence of God and all that are of Him with that which shows sin and evil and shows and knows you to be for destruction and condemnation in the lake that burns. This limits your liberty and cuts it short. The liberty of the sons of God [not] you nor none of your spirit shall ever know, which is purchased by Jesus Christ, who you are a crucifier of, and an enemy to. This was the liberty the apostle exhorts to stand fast in, which binds and chains you and condemns you. Who is in this liberty sees you the devil's bondslave. What is in God you know not. Neither know you what God is. You are under the sun, the moon, and the stars, lying wallowing in your earthly lust and uncleanness. The earth is cursed for your sake. The living God has cursed you above all the beasts of the field.

RANTERS: One counsel orders all and one wisdom effects and determines all and of one all learn knowledge and wisdom. This counsel nothing resists. This counsel were they ordered by, who crucified the Son of God.

ANSWER: You are the rebellious, stiff necked, and uncircumcised who are not ordered by the counsel of the Lord. In that you say, one counsel orders all. You are a liar and the Lord witnesses against you: "Therefore the Lord was angry with Amaziah and sent to him a prophet, who said to him, 'Why have you resorted to the gods of a people, which did not deliver their own people from your hand?' But as he was speaking the king said to him, 'Have we made you a royal counselor? Stop! Why should you be put to death?' So the prophet stopped, but said, 'I know that God has determined to destroy you, because you have done this and have not listened to my counsel'" (2 Chron. 25:15-16). Here is the King's Counsel and God's Counsel. Solomon says,[16] "Because I have called and you refused to listen, have stretched out my hand and no one has heeded, and you have ignored all my counsel and would have none of my reproof, I also will laugh at your calamity; I will mock when panic strikes you, when panic strikes you like a storm, and your calamity comes like a whirlwind, when distress and anguish come upon you. Then they will call upon me, but I will not answer; they will seek me diligently but will not find me. Because they hated knowledge and did not choose the fear of the Lord, would have none of my counsel, and despised all my reproof, therefore they shall eat the fruit of their way and be sated with their own devices" (Prov. 1:24-31). You are one of the wicked counselors that do imagine evil against the Lord. He will make an utter end of you and all of your spirit. Though you be folded together as thorns and are drunken as drunkards, you shall be devoured as stubble fully dry. "Did one not come out from you, who plotted evil against the Lord, and counseled villainy?" (Nah. 1:11). You have made it manifest that you are one of them that took counsel together to put him to death. You, who crucifies Him, rejects His counsel (Luke 7:30). Your wisdom is carnal, sensual, and devilish (James 3:15; 1 Cor. 1:19). By the wisdom of God, you and your wisdom shall be destroyed.

RANTERS: He that has faith and liberty to do all things, to him nothing is unclean nor unlawful. To him, everything is pure.

ANSWER: You have liberty to do all things which are unclean, filthy, and polluted, and are without faith. Your liberty is bondage. From the living God, you are driven under the curse and bondage of corruption. You that are servants to sin are free from righteousness (Rom. 6:20). To you who are in the lust of uncleanness, [to you who] act by the dark power, and to you who are unclean and impure, nothing is pure, whose conscience is defiled. You bring a scripture in Titus 1:15 where it is said, "To the pure all things are pure…." Oh, you blasphemer, what is this to you who are defiled and filthy? Do not the apostle's words follow: "…but to the corrupt and unbelieving nothing is pure; their very minds and consciences are corrupted. They profess to know God, but they deny him by their deeds; they are detestable, disobedient, unfit for any good deed." There you are.

RANTERS: The seed of the serpent is cursed and no blessing belongs to it. The seed of God, God will save. God will save His own. What does man's doing advantage him or not doing disadvantage him?

ANSWER: Here, you serpent [you] have made yourself manifest to be the cursed seed indeed, who has twined and twisted about, tempting into sin and transgression all your paper[17] through, and pleaded for lust, filthiness, and uncleanness, and liberty of the flesh, which lusts against the spirit. Now at last you have uttered forth your blasphemy and confusion and laid yourself open to all. If you will have two seeds, the seed of the serpent and the seed of God: In this, you have overturned and confounded all that ever you have spoken in your paper before. So you are judged out of your own mouth. All that you have pleaded for, you have overturned by this.[18]

Before you said God was darkness as well as light, both being alike to him, and all acted by one power, and good and evil one, and sin and holiness one, and all things that be are wrought by one wisdom. [You] said invention is found out by that wisdom, whatsoever has been done in darkness may be done in the light, and that God loves and takes pleasure in all things.

Now you say the seed of the serpent is cursed. These are your own words: Here you are found with lies and confusion in your mouth and so, you serpent, [you] are cursed. All lying is of the devil. He is the father of all these blasphemies that you have uttered. Your actings do not advantage for you to treasure up wrath against the day of wrath. The wrath of the Lord God will find you out and the plagues of God you shall witness, for they are your portion.

You and some of your spirit have said that there was nothing between your Ranters and the Quakers—only they did not see all things to be theirs, so were in bondage, but they would grow up to you.

Those whom you call Quakers do utterly deny you and all of your principles. All the Ranters are by us denied. Your practices we abhor. In the eternal light which never changes do we see you and know you. With that which was before the world was, do we try your spirits and comprehend your bottom and foundation and race you out from the presence of the Lord and all who are of Him. In the dread and power of the living God, do we judge and try you and your god, which is the god of the world and the prince of the air which now is come to be judged. [We] do judge and condemn both him and you into the lake which burns.

This is from the Quakers which you say are not yet come to you, but are from you separated eternally.

Margaret Fell

CHAPTER 5

MARGARET FELL FOX IN HER OWN WORDS

Historical and Content Introduction

The following section contains four key documents from Margaret Fell concerning herself: her mysterious first letter to George Fox, two autobiographical remembrances written in her last years, and a brief summary of her deathbed witness. All but the first letter give us a remarkable self-portrait—straight-forward, unemotional, starkly unembellished—in fact, written in the plainest of plain styles. We find neither the wild emotionalism of the religious enthusiast nor the self-aggrandizing pride of the memoirist. Only Fell's first letter fails to fit this description at first reading. But there may be a plausible explanation for it, one better than "religious enthusiasm"—the explanation offered by scholars of years past.

The Mystery Letter

The first letter Margaret Fell wrote to George Fox after her convincement is included here, because it seems a marked anomaly (and a much remarked upon one) in comparison to the rest of her writing.

The first half of the letter addresses Fox in terms so startlingly messianic in tone ("O you bread of life," "O you fountain of eternal life," "O you father of eternal felicity") so emotional in tenor, that we must conclude the writer, or writers, were in a state of confused enthusiasm. Isabel Ross' gentle characterization of the document is representative of the scholarly reading of Margaret's spiritual state and evolution: "Perhaps her zeal for the new teaching showed in the very early days a little too much emotionalism...but this soon deepened and passed away" [p. 36]. Ross asserts Margaret Fell moved in six months from confused enthusiasm to a spiritual and emotional maturity that made her the rock solid Mother of Quakerism. Her overemotional enthusiasm "never recurred" [p. 38]. A brief reading of Margaret's letter at first glance appears to bear out this interpretation.

However, when one reviews the circumstances under which the letter was written and does a closer reading of the document itself, another possible interpretation emerges. The occasion for the letter was Fox's unhappy departure from Swarthmoor, accompanied by his ominous biblical "shaking the dust" from his feet, because one of the men in the household refused to hear and receive his words.

Exactly when this event occurred is more difficult, but not impossible to establish. The situation is complicated by the fact that Fox made several visits to Swarthmoor at the end of June and during the month of July, 1652, the period of general convincement for Fell, her family, and household. Fox's first arrival at Swarthmoor, as June ended, occasioned several confrontations with the rector of Ulverston's steeple house, William Lampitt. However, since he was neither a member of the household nor ever convinced of the Truth, he was clearly not the motivation for Fox's departure.

In fact, by the evening of Thursday, July 1, Fell and her household were well on their way to convincement. Within the next few days Fox moved up and down the peninsula in ministry, circling more than once back to Swarthmoor close to the center of that arm of land. After a Sunday, July 4, in Aldingham, he returned briefly to Swarthmoor. On Sunday, July 11, he moved down the peninsula further, first to Dalton, then to Walney Island off the coast, then back to Swarthmoor, where he found Fell and many in the household growing in convincement. However, between July 11 and the last week of the month, when Judge Fell returned to his wife and home after riding the Welsh Circuit, Fox absented himself from Swarthmoor for nearly two weeks and left the peninsula moving through Kendal and Sedbergh.

Furthermore, Fell reports her own state of mind as "under great heaviness and judgment" when "two weeks after" Fox's first visit, James Nayler and Richard Farnsworth (Quaker ministers traveling in Fox's wake and seeking his present whereabouts) arrived at Swarthmoor. While her heaviness and judgment—the initial conviction of one's failure to do God's will—was a typical early phase of Quaker convincement in the seventeenth century, it is possible that Fell's and the household's spiritual state of mind was aggravated by Fox's refusal to remain. Fell reports Nayler's and Farnsworth's stay at Swarthmoor "did me much good" and Judge Fell's return and acceptance of his radically altered household became the central focus of her concern. The two weeks before Fox's return appear to be the period we are seeking. Fell's state of mind was heavy. Fox was headed distinctly out of the region. A letter was clearly needed to call him back.

The internal structure and changes of tone which we find in the letter are significant to its correct interpretation. The document is divided into two sections. The first was jointly composed by members of the household with Margaret Fell's assistance as amanuensis (i.e., taking dictation). The composition is somewhat disjointed, redundant, plaintive, and at times childish in character, and perhaps close to hysterical in a line or two. The first section ends first with four individual pleas from Fell's younger daughters,[1] followed by the signatures of Fell and the rest of the family and household. Mary Fell's, "You are the fountain of life," is significant, for it echoes the, "Oh, you fountain of eternal life," near the close of the first section. Susan and Sarah Fell address Fox as "father"—an appellation in marked use in the first section of the letter. None of these terms, nor the flagrant language of the first section, appear in Margaret Fell's personal section.

Fell's addition to the letter is far more subdued. Rather than plaintive and uncontrolled, it is a carefully worded, coherent argument to Fox to come back and finish his work. The one repeated appellation is "dear heart." It exhorts him "to strike down the deceit." If he refuses, he will be not only adding much "to our sorrow," but bolstering "the beastly power." While the language is tense, Fell knows precisely the arguments that will reach Fox. Her case is as pointed and mature as her later works. Nowhere in her plea does she fall into the obviously confused language of the first section.

In brief, then, the letter reflects two different states of mind. The first—confused, grieved, nearly hysterical—reflects the state of the household and the younger members of the Fell family. The voices of the first section are the voices of children, one after the other, adding their pleas and complaints. Fell's hand in its composition seems mainly therapeutic, allowing the shaken young members to vent their anguish. She signs the section with her children and household as a responsible parent would, demonstrating the profound importance she attached to their spiritual concern, growth, and welfare.

However, the second section is obviously Margaret Fell speaking. Clear, definite, and pointed, it is consistent with the Fell we see later, the Fell who was already Fox's senior by ten years, the Fell who at the age of thirty-eight in 1652 is responsible for running an estate of significant size, raising both a large family and overseeing its attendant household staff. Such a reading of the letter is clearly more in line with the personality of the shrewd, astute woman who had already been married to Judge Fell for twenty years and who would serve fifty more as "the nursing mother of Quakerism." The supposed aberration in her personality in 1652—an aberration never seen before or after July, 1652, may simply be a scholarly creation based on a misreading of the document.

A Relation and A Testimony

"A Relation of Margaret Fell" is Fell's fullest autobiographical account. However, two others exist: (1) "The Testimony of Margaret Fox Concerning Her Late Husband George Fox..." prefacing the 1694 first edition of Fox's *Journal* and (2) a rough draft of an introduction to an unpublished collection of letters, part of the Spence Manuscripts (see specifically Spence MSS 111:135f). The first two volumes of the Spence Manuscripts contain the original *Journal of George Fox*. Volume three is largely composed of letters by Margaret Fell.

"A Relation" was the first of these documents to be composed, Fell herself dating it the 10th day of 7th Month, 1690. She was then seventy-six years of age and had just completed her ninth visit to London (each round trip from Swarthmoor covered a distance of more than 400 miles). It would be the final time she saw Fox alive, for—as she clearly details in her "Testimony"—both of them felt the Lord called them to service in different places: she at Swarthmoor in the North, he in London.

"The Testimony" of Fell for her husband's *Journal* was composed in the months following Fox's death in January of 1691. The account shows the journey to London and her earlier "Relation" were much on her mind, for the London visit is remembered in similar positive terms, as the "most comfortable" of the nine visits and as having "the Lord's special hand...in it." Further, each account supplements the other with relatively little unnecessary overlap, the major difference between the two being one of focus. "The Testimony" is obviously a witness to, and remembrance of, Fox and his work.

"A Relation" is especially valuable for giving us some insight into Margaret Fell's first marriage, her religious state before Fox appeared on the scene, her sufferings for the Gospel, her significant ministry, and her lobbying work in London. We find Fell's profound religious concern existed long before the arrival of Quakers on her doorstep.

Moreover, her suspicion that she remained "short of the right way" in spite of all her religious observances explains her remarkable response to Fox's preaching in the Ulverston steeple house, as related in her "Testimony."

Fell's own account also captures well the various persecutions suffered by Friends and herself, from early violence and imprisonments to later economic attacks in the 1680s. Along with notes on persecution, Fell describes in some detail the Quaker lobbying efforts with government officials, efforts that often found her a central participant. Unlike modern Quaker efforts, however, Margaret Fell's went far beyond immediate mundane political goals and challenged the Government with the Good News that Christ Jesus "is come to teach and lead his people today." The Quaker efforts described are remarkably systematic and thorough, but—unlike the partisan politics and subtle maneuvers of the modern lobbyist—always carried forward with an eye to Truth and unflinching honesty.

"The Testimony" supplements "A Relation" in two important areas: Fell's convincement is reviewed in detail and her marriage to George Fox receives clarification and defense. If we had only Fell's "A Relation" to go on, we could come away feeling she was remarkably unenthusiastic about her second marriage. Even Fox's accounts in his *Journal* are more fulsome. Yet, even in "The Testimony," the Fox/Fell union seems notably businesslike. Within weeks of their marriage, we find Fox "intending" to travel in America, a journey of two years. Imprisonment and ministry consumed their years and we find Fox and Fell most often together when Fox is incapacitated by illness. The close of Fell's "Testimony" provides clear evidence that some remarked negatively at their rather unusual relationship.

Yet, three things should be kept in mind. First, by mutual agreement, both Fox and Fell were clear that the demands of God and His service came first in their lives. Fell stoutly identifies this as the sole reason for their long periods apart. Second, both of Margaret Fell's marriages are similar in this respect. We must remember that Judge Fell's judicial duties and circuit left her at the head of her household for weeks at a time. Her twenty-six years of marriage to Judge Fell and eleven years of widowhood and imprisonment had left her as tempered as hard steel. She had no problem with being self-sufficient and independent. The novelist Jan de Hartog's portrait, in his *The Peaceable Kingdom*, of a Margaret Fell romantically swept away by Fox's sexual charisma, is a figment of twentieth century imagination. Finally, the myth of romantic love, a staple of twentieth century relationships, found no significant root in seventeenth century England. The relationships of that era were guided by far more practical concerns and enduring values.

The Last Words

The compilation of Margaret Fell's last words, in this section, originally prefaced the volume of her works in London in 1710, *A Brief Collection of Remarkable Passages and Occurrences....* It stood there as both a first and final testimony of Truth. The last sayings of those about to die were considered of high importance, not only among Quakers, but among men and women in general, for the moment of death was the final test and tribulation of faith. The King of Terrors, as death was sometimes called, was a frightful separator of those of chaffy faith from those whose trust was firm. Fell's words serve well as a strong seal to a strong life in the service of Christ. She dies weak in body at the advanced age of eighty-eight, but clearly at rest in the will of God, at peace and comfortable—concerned only that her children and grandchildren stand strong in the faith.

Her passing on April 23, 1702, is the closing event in the history of the first Publishers of Truth, that first generation of Quakers who proclaimed so forcefully and faithfully the continuing revelation of Christ. Most of the Valiant Sixty, those early, intrepid Quaker ministers who fanned out across England and the world with their message, had laid down their lives by 1680, most in prisons and as sufferers for their faith. George Fox's remarkably robust strength had been spent by 1691. Only Margaret Fell lived on to witness the Society of Friends turning progressively away from the Lamb's War with the world, away from the universal proclamation of its Everlasting Gospel, and away from the freedom of the Spirit towards a regimented legalism. Yet, she is clear in her own service to her Lord and quiets those who grieve at her passing with the declaration that she is "as comfortable, and well in my spirit, as ever I was."

The Mystery Letter

For GF

Our dear father in the Lord, for though we have ten-thousand instructors in Christ, yet have we not many fathers, for in Christ Jesus, you have begotten us through the gospel. Eternal praise be to our father. We are your babes with one consent being gathered together in the power of the Spirit, you being present with us. Our souls do thirst and languish after you, and challenge that right that we have in you. If you bread of life, without which bread our souls will starve—oh for evermore give us this bread. Take pity on us, whom you have nursed up with the breasts of consolation. Oh, our life, our desires are to see you again that we may be refreshed and established and so have life more abundantly. Let not that beastly power which keeps us in bondage separate your bodily presence, who reigns as king above it, from us. [We] would rejoice to see your kingly power here triumph over it. Oh, our dear nursing father, we hope you will not leave us comfortless, but will come again. Though that sorrow be for a time, yet joy comes in the morning. Oh, our life, we hope to see you again, that our joy may be full, for in your presence is fullness of joy. Where you dwell are pleasures for evermore. Oh, you fountain of eternal life, our souls thirst after you, for in you alone is our life and peace. Without you have we no peace, for our souls are much refreshed by seeing you. Our lives are preserved by you, O you father of eternal felicity.

O, my dear father, when will you come? —Susan Fell

Dear father, pray for us. —Sarah Fell

Oh, my dear heart, shall we not see you ever more again? —Issabell Fell

Thou art the fountain of life. —Mary Fell

Margaret Fell
Tho. Salthouse
Ann Clayton
Mary Askew
Bridgett Fell
Will. Caton

My own dear heart, though you have shaken the dust of your foot at him who would not receive you, and is not worthy of you—which shall be a testimony against him forever—yet you know that we have received you into our hearts, and shall live with you eternally. It is our life and joy to be with you. So, my heart, let not the power of darkness separate your bodily presence from us, which will be a grief and trouble to us, and especially through him, whom you know can call nothing his own but the plagues and woes.

My soul thirsts to have you to come over, if it be but for two or three days, to strike down the deceit in him for the truth's sake.

And if you do not come, it will add abundantly to our sorrow and strengthen the beastly power. I know it is a burden and suffering to you, but you have borne our burdens and suffered for us and with us. Now, dear heart, do not leave us nor forsake us, for our life and power are in you.

M.F. 1652.

[From the reverse side of the letter—a later, additional note]

This was sent to G.F. and he came back again to we that sent for him, and he, that he shaked the dust off his feet against, was not long after convinced.

A Relation of Margaret Fell
Her Birth, Life, Testimony, and Sufferings for the Lord's Everlasting Truth in Her Generation

Given forth by herself, as follows:

I was born in the year 1614 at Marsh-Grange, in the parish of Dalton, in Fournis in Lancashire, of good and honest parents, of honorable repute in their country. My father's name was John Askew. He was of an ancient family, of those esteemed and called Gentlemen, who left a considerable estate which had been in his name and family for several generations. He was a pious charitable man, much valued in his country for his moderation and patience, and was bred after the best way and manner of persons of his rank in his day. I was brought up and lived with my father until I was between seventeen and eighteen years of age. Then I was married unto Thomas Fell of Swarthmoor who was a barrister at law of Grays Inn, who afterwards was a Justice of the Quorum in his country, a Member of Parliament in several Parliaments, Vice Chancellor of the County Palatine of Lancaster, Chancellor of the Dutchy Court at Westminster, and one of the judges that went the circuit of West Chester and North Wales.

He was much esteemed in his country, valued and honored in his day by all sorts of people for his justice, wisdom, moderation, and mercy, being a terror to evil doers and an encourager of such as did well. His many and great services made his death much lamented. We lived together twenty-six years, in which time we had nine children. He was a tender loving husband to me, a tender father to his children, and one that sought after God in the best way that was made known to him. I was about sixteen years younger than he, was one that sought after the best things, being desirous to serve God (so as I might be accepted of Him), was inquiring after the way of the Lord, and went often to hear the best ministers that came into our parts, whom we frequently entertained at our house. Many of those were accounted the most serious and godly men, some of whom were then called Lecturing Ministers,[1] and had often prayers and religious exercises in our family. This I hoped I did well in, but often feared I was short of the right way. After this manner, I was inquiring and seeking about twenty years.

In the year 1652, it pleased the Lord in his infinite mercy and goodness to send George Fox into our country,[2] who declared unto us the eternal truth as it is in Jesus and by the word and power of the eternal God turned many from darkness unto light, from the power of Satan unto God. [This was] when I, my children, and a great part of our servants were so convinced and converted unto God, at which time my husband was not at home, being gone to London. When he came home and found us the most part of the family changed from our former principle and persuasion which he left us in when he went from home, he was much surprised at our sudden change, for some envious people of our neighbors went and met him upon the Sands,[3] as he was coming home, and informed him that we had entertained such men as had taken us off from going to church—which he was very much concerned at, so that when he came home, he seemed much troubled. It so happened that Richard Farnsworth and some other Friends (that came into our parts a little time after G. Fox) were then at our house when my husband came home. They discoursed with him and did persuade him to be still, weigh things before he did anything hastily, and his spirit was something calmed.

At night, G. Fox spoke so powerfully and convincingly that the witness of God in his [Judge Fell's] conscience answered that he spoke the truth. He was then so far convinced in his mind that it was truth, that he willingly let us have a Meeting in his house the next First Day after, which was the first public Meeting that was at Swarthmoor. Yet, he and his men went to the steeple house (our Meetings being kept at Swarthmoor about thirty-eight years until a new meetinghouse was built, by G. Fox's order and cost, near Swarthmoor Hall). So, through the good power and words of God, the truth increased in the countries all about us. Many came in and were convinced. We kept our Meetings peaceably every First Day at Swarthmoor Hall, the residue of the time of his life. He became a kind friend to Friends and to the practicers of truth upon every occasion, as he had opportunity, for he being a magistrate[4] was instrumental to keep off much persecution in this country and in other places where he had any power.

He lived about six years after I was convinced, in which time it pleased the Lord to visit him with sickness, wherein he became more than usually loving and kind to our Friends called Quakers, having been a merciful man to the Lord's people. I and many other Friends were satisfied the Lord in mercy received him to Himself. It was in the beginning of the 10th month, 1658, that he died, being about sixty years of age. He left one son, and seven daughters all unpreferred,[5] but left a good and competent estate for them.

In the year 1660, King Charles the Second came into England. Within two weeks after, I was moved of the Lord to go to London, to speak to the King concerning the truth and the sufferers for it, for there were then many hundreds of our Friends in prison in the three nations of England, Scotland, and Ireland, which were put in by the former powers.[6] I spoke often with the King, wrote many letters and papers unto him (and many books were given by our Friends to the Parliament), and great service was done at that time.[7] They were fully informed of our peaceable principles and practices.[8] I stayed at London at this time one year and three months, doing service for the Lord in visiting Friends Meetings and giving papers and letters to the King and Council whenever there was occasion. I wrote and gave papers and letters to every one of the [royal] family several times, viz., to the King, to the Duke of York, to the Duke of Gloucester, to the Queen Mother, to the Princess of Orange, and to the Queen of Bohemia. I was moved of the Lord to visit them all, to write unto them, to lay the truth before them, and did give them many books and papers, did lay our principles and doctrines before them, and desired that they would let us have discourse with their priests, preachers, and teachers. If they could prove us erroneous, then let them manifest it. But if our principles and doctrines be found according to the doctrine of Christ, the apostles and saints in the primitive times, then let us have our liberty. But we could never get a meeting of any sort of them to meet with our Friends. Nevertheless, they were very quiet.

We had great liberty and had our Meetings very peaceably for the first half year after the King came in, until the Fifth Monarchy Men raised an insurrection and tumult in the city of London. Then all our Meetings were disturbed and Friends were taken up, which [insurrection] if that had not been, we were informed the King had intended to have given us liberty. For at that very time, there was an order signed by the King and Council for the Quakers' liberty. Just when it should have gone to the press, the Fifth Monarchy Men rose. Then our Friends were very hardly used and taken up at their Meetings generally, even until many prisons throughout the nation were filled with them.

Many a time did I go to the King about them, who promised me always they should be set at liberty. We had several in the Council [who] were friendly to us. We gave many papers to them. With much ado and attendance in that time, about a quarter of a year after their first taking Friends to prison, a General Proclamation from the King and Council was granted for setting the Quakers at liberty that were taken up at that time. In some time after, the Proclamation came forth and Friends were set at liberty. Then I had freedom in spirit to return home to visit my children and family, whom I had been from fifteen months.

I stayed at home about nine months and then was moved of the Lord to go to London again, not knowing what might be the matter or business that I should go for. When I came to Warrington in my way to London, I met with an act of Parliament made against the Quakers for refusing oaths. When I came to London, I heard the King was gone to meet the Queen and to be married to her at Hampton Court. At this time Friends Meetings at London were much troubled with soldiers pulling Friends out of their Meetings, beating them with their muskets and swords insomuch that several were wounded and bruised by them. Many were cast into prison, through which many lost their lives, all this being done to a peaceable people, only for worshiping God as they in conscience were persuaded. Then I went to the King and Duke of York at Hampton Court. I wrote several letters to them and therein gave them to understand what desperate and dangerous work there was at London: how the soldiers came in with lighted matches and drawn swords among Friends when they were met together in the fear and dread of the Lord to worship Him. If they would not stop that cruel persecution, it was very likely that more innocent blood would be shed, and that would witness against their actions and lie upon them and the nation. Within some certain days after, they beat some Friends so cruelly, at the Bull and Mouth, that two died thereof.

The King told me when I spoke to him and wrote to him that his soldiers did not trouble us nor should they, and said the city soldiers were not his and they would do as they pleased with them. Yet, after a little time, they were more moderate. The King promised me that he would set those at liberty that were in prison. When he brought his Queen to London, he set them at liberty. Then I came home again, when I had stayed about four months in and about London.

In the 5th month, 1663, I was moved of the Lord again to travel into the countries to visit Friends, and I traveled through the countries visiting Friends till we came to Bristol where we stayed two weeks—I and some other Friends that were with me. Then we went to Somersetshire, Devonshire, and Dorsetshire, visiting Friends, and came back to Bristol. From whence, we passed through the nation into Yorkshire, to York, into Bishoprick and North Umberland visiting Meetings all along amongst Friends, and then went into Westmorland and so home to Swarthmoor.

[On] this journey that I then went (and one of my daughters and some others that were with me), it was thought we traveled about a thousand miles.[9]

In our journey, we met with G. Fox, who came to Swarthmoor with us and stayed about two weeks. Then the magistrates began to threaten: for G.F. went into Westmorland and Cumberland, and had some Meetings amongst Friends, and came again to Swarthmoor. They sent out warrants for him, took him, and committed him to Lancaster Castle.[10] About a month after, the same Justices sent for me to Alverstone where they were sitting at a private Sessions. When I came there, they asked me several questions, seemed to be offended at me for keeping a Meeting at my house, and said they would tender me the Oath of Allegiance. I answered they knew I could not swear. Why should they send for me from my own house, where I was about my lawful occasions, to ensnare me? What had I done? They said if I would not keep a Meeting at my house, they would not tender me the Oath. I told them I should not deny my faith and principles for anything they could do against me, and while it pleased the Lord to let me have a house, I would endeavor to worship Him in it. So they caused the Oath to be read and tendered it unto me. When I refused it, [I told] them I could not take any Oath for conscience's sake, Christ Jesus having forbid it. Then they made a Mittimus and committed me prisoner to Lancaster Castle. There G. Fox and I remained in prison until the next Assizes. Then they indicted us upon the statute for denying the Oath of Allegiance, for they tendered it us both again at the Assizes (but they said to me, if I would not keep a Meeting at my house, I should be set at liberty). But I answered the Judge, "That I rather choose a prison for obeying of God, than my liberty for obeying of men contrary to my conscience." So we were called several times before them at that Assizes. The indictments were found against us.

The next Assizes we came to trial and G. Fox's indictment was found to be dated wrong, both in the day of the month, and in the year of the King's reign, so that his indictment was quashed. Mine they would not allow the errors that were found in it, to make it void, although there were several. So, they passed sentence of praemunire upon me which was that I should be out of the King's protection, forfeit all my estate real and personal to the King, and [bear] imprisonment during life. But the great God of heaven and earth supported my spirit under this severe sentence, that I was not terrified, but gave this answer to Judge Turner who gave the sentence: "Although I am out of the King's protection, yet I am not out of the protection of the Almighty God." So there I remained in prison twenty months, before I could get so much favor of the sheriff as to go to my house, which then I did for a little time and returned to prison again. When I had been a prisoner for about four years, I was set at liberty by an order from the King and Council in 1668.[11]

Then I was moved of the Lord again to go and visit Friends. The first that I went to visit were Friends in prison. I visited the most part of the Friends that were prisoners in the North and West of England, and those on my way to Bristol. After I had stayed two weeks there, I visited Friends in Cornwall, Devonshire, and Somersetshire, and then through all the western counties to London. I stayed in and about London about three months. Then I went and visited friends throughout all Kent, Sussex, and some part of Surrey, and then to London again where I stayed above two months. Then I returned through the countries, visiting Friends until I came to Bristol in 1669.

Then it was eleven years after my former husband's decease, and G. Fox being then returned from visiting Friends in Ireland. At Bristol, he declared his intentions of marriage with me. There was also our marriage solemnized in a public Meeting of many friends who were our witnesses.[12]

In some time after, I came homewards and my husband stayed in the countries visiting Friends. Soon after I came home, there came another order to cast me into prison again. The sheriff of Lancashire sent his bailiff, pulled me out of my own house, and had me to prison to Lancaster Castle where I continued a whole year and most part of that time I was sick and weakly. After some time, my husband endeavored to get me out of prison. A discharge at last was got, under the Great Seal, and so I was set at liberty.[13]

Then I was to go up to London again, for my husband was intending for America. He was full two years away, before he came back to England. Then he arrived in Bristol where I went to meet him. We stayed sometime in the countries thereabout, then came to London, and stayed there several months. I was intending to return home into the North. He came with me as far as the middle of the nation. But before we parted, we went to a Meeting in Worcestershire. After the Meeting was ended and Friends mostly gone, he was taken prisoner, together with my son-in-law Thomas Lower, and sent to Worcester jail by one Parker, a Justice so called (the account whereof is set forth in his *Journal*).[14] I came home with my daughter Rachel, leaving him confined in prison where he became much weakened in body and his health impaired by his long confinement. Howbeit, after much endeavor used, he was legally discharged and set at liberty. We got him home to Swarthmoor where he had a long time of weakness before he recovered. When he had stayed there about one and twenty months, he began his journey towards London again in 1677. Although he was but weakly and unable to ride well, the Lord supported him. When he had stayed some time in London, then he went over into Holland, traveled to Hamburg, into some part of Germany, to several places in those countries, then returned to London, then went to Bristol to visit Friends, and back again to London. Then, after a little time, [he] came to Swarthmoor, where he continued again above a year. Then he began his journey and traveled through several countries visiting Friends, until he came to London.[15]

When my husband was at London, it being a time of great persecution by informers,[16] the Justices in our country were very severe and much bent against me because I kept a Meeting at my house at Swarthmoor Hall. So they did not fine the house as his, he being absent, but fined it as mine as being the widow of Judge Fell, fined me twenty pounds for the house, twenty pounds for speaking in the Meeting, then fined me the second time forty pounds for speaking. [They] also fined some other Friends for speaking, twenty pounds for the first time, forty pounds for the second time, and those that were not able, they fined others for them, and made great spoil among Friends by distraining and selling their goods, sometimes for less than half the value. They took thirty head of cattle from me. Their intentions were to ruin us, to weary us out, and to enrich themselves, but the Lord prevented them.

So I was moved of the Lord to go to London in the seventieth year of my age. The word was in me, "That as I had gone to King Charles when he first came into England, so I should go, and bear to him my last testimony, and let him know how they did abuse us to enrich themselves." So I went up to London and a paper was drawn up to give a true and certain account, how they dealt with me and other Friends. It was upon my mind to go first to the Duke of York. I wrote a short paper to him to acquaint him, that as he had sometimes formerly spoke in my behalf to the King, my request was that they would now do the like for me—or words to that effect. I went with this paper to James' house. After long waiting, I got to speak to him. But some who were with him let him know that it was I that had been with him and his brother soon after they came into England. So I gave him my little paper and asked him if he did remember me? He said, "I do remember you." So then I desired him to speak to the King for us, for we were under great sufferings. Our persecutors were so severe upon us that it looked as if they intended to make a prey upon us. He said, he could not help us, but he would speak to the King. The next day, with much ado, I got to the King and had my great paper, which was the relation of our sufferings, to present to him, but he was so rough and angry that he would not take my paper (but I gave several copies of it to his nobles about him). Afterwards I went to Judge Jefferies and told him of our sufferings, for he had been in the North Country with us but a little before. He told me we might speak to the King. I answered, it was very hard to get to the King. He said, "Give me a paper and I will speak to him," but said, "Your papers are too long. Give me a short paper and I will speak to him." So I wrote a little paper from myself to him to this effect: "King Charles, you and your magistrates put very great and cruel sufferings upon us. This I must say unto you: If you make our suffering to death itself, we shall not, nor dare not but confess Christ Jesus before men, lest he should deny us before his Father which is in heaven."

There were some more words in it, but this was the substance. So Jefferies read it and said he would give it to him. We gave papers to several of those that waited on him. They gave us some encouragement, that we should be helped. So we expected and waited for it. About a week or two after, in the beginning of the 2nd month, George Whitehead and I were going to one of the Lords who had promised George before that he would speak to the King for us. We went to his lodgings early in the morning, thinking to speak with him before he went out, but his servants told us he was not within, being gone to the King who was not well. Then we came forth into White Hall Court again, but all the gates were shut, that we could not get forth. So we waited and walked up and down. Several came down from the King and said, "He could not stand." Others said, "He could not speak." Then, after some hours waiting, we got through Scotland Yard and came away. The King continued sick and ill until the sixth day after. Then he died. So this confirmed that word, which God put into my heart: that I was sent to bear my last testimony to the King.

Then James, Duke of York, was proclaimed King. About two weeks after, I went to him and gave him a paper wherein was written to this effect: "King James, I have waited here some months, until this change is come. Now I would return home, but I cannot live peaceably there, except I have a word from you to give a check to my persecutors." I spoke to him to the same purpose that I had written in my paper. He said to me, "Go home. Go home." So after a few weeks, I went home.

A little time after, William Kirkby, a Justice, one of our greatest persecutors, met with my son-in-law, Daniel Abraham, upon the road and said to him, "Tell your mother that now the government will be settled again and, if you keep Meetings, you must expect the same again." My son answered him, "We must keep Meetings, unless you take our lives." Then William Kirkby said, "We will not take your lives, but while you have anything, we will take it." So I wrote a letter to King James, in which I said, "You bid me come home and so I am, but as I said to you, I could not live peaceably, so it is like to be." Then I hinted in my letter W. Kirkby's discourse with my son. I desired of the King, "to let me have something from him, that I might live peaceably at my house."

This letter was delivered to him, and, as I heard, he carried it to the Council. It was read and some in the Council said, "She desires a protection,[17] that she may live peaceably at her own house;" and some said they could give no protection to a particular. However, (I do suppose) they gave our persecutors a private caution, for they troubled us no more. If that had not been, it's likely they had a mind to begin anew upon us. A little before the time of the informers,[18] they brought the law upon us concerning the pence a Sunday, so called. They carried me and my son and daughter Abraham to Lancaster Prison and kept us there about three weeks. When they considered that they could not fine me nor my house when I was in prison, they let us go home. Soon after, they did fine us both for the house and for speaking, as it before hinted.

Thus have they troubled and persecuted us diverse ways. But the Lord God Almighty has preserved me and us till this day: glorious praises be given to Him for evermore.

The Lord has given me strength and ability that I have been at London to see my dear husband and children, relations and Friends there, in 1690, being the seventy-sixth year of my age. I was very well satisfied, refreshed, and comforted in my journey, and found Friends in much love. Praises be returned to the unchangeable Lord God forever. This being nine times that I have been at London, upon the Lord's and His truth's account.

After I returned home, I wrote this short epistle following to the Women's Meetings in London:

Dear Friends and Sisters,

In the eternal blessed truth, into which we are begotten and in which we stand and are preserved as we keep in it and are guided by it: In this is my dear and unchangeable love remembered unto you all, acknowledging your dear, tender, and kind love when I was with you—in which my heart rejoiced to feel the ancient love and unity of the eternal Spirit among you. My soul was and is refreshed in my journey, in visiting of my dear husband and children, and you my dear Friends. Now I am returned to my own house and family where I find all well. Praised and honored be my heavenly Father.

Dear Friends, our engagements are great unto the Lord. He is dear and faithful unto us. Blessed and happy are all they that are dear and faithful unto Him. Those who keep single and chaste unto Him: they need not fear evil tidings nor what man can do, for He that has all power in heaven and earth in His hand—He will surely keep his own church and family, those that worshipped Him within the measuring line that measures the temple, the altar, and those that worship therein. They are kept safe, as in the hollow of His hand.

So, dear Friends, my heart and soul were so much comforted and refreshed among you that I could not but signify the remembrance of my dear love unto you, and also my acknowledgment of your dear love and tenderness to my dear husband—for which I doubt not, but the Lord does and will reward you. Into whose hand, and arm, and power, I commit you.

Swarthmoor, the 10th of the 7th month, 1690.
Margaret Fell

The Testimony of Margaret Fox Concerning Her Late Husband George Fox, Together with a Brief Account of Some of His Travels, Sufferings, and Hardships Endured for the Truth's Sake[1]

It having pleased Almighty God to take away my dear husband out of this evil, troublesome world, who was not a man thereof, being chosen out of it, and [who] had his life and being in another region, and his testimony was against the world, that the deeds thereof were evil, and therefore the world hated him: So I am now to give in my account and testimony for my dear husband, who the Lord has taken unto his blessed kingdom and glory. It is before me from the Lord, and in my view, to give a relation, and leave upon record the dealings of the Lord with us from the beginning.

He was the instrument in the hand of the Lord in this present age, which he made use of to send forth into the world, to preach the Everlasting Gospel, which had been hid from many ages and generations. The Lord revealed it unto him, and made him open that new and living way, that leads to life eternal, when he was but a youth and a stripling. When he declared it in his own country of Leicestershire, and in Darbyshire, Nottinghamshire, and Warwickshire, his declaration being against the hireling priests and their practices, it raised a great fury and opposition among the priests and people against him. Yet there were always some that owned him in several places, but very few that stood firm to him, when persecution came on him. There was he and one other put in Derby, but the other declined and left him in prison there, where he continued almost a whole year. Then he was released out of prison and went on with his testimony abroad and was put in prison again in Nottingham.[2] There he continued a while and after was released again.

Then he traveled on into Yorkshire, passed up and down that great county, and several received him, [such] as William Dewsbury, Richard Farnsworth, Thomas Aldam, and others who all came to be faithful ministers of the Spirit of the Lord. He continued in that country, traveled through Holderness and the Wolds, and abundance were convinced. Several were brought to prison at York for their testimony to the truth, both men and women, so that we heard of such a people that were risen. We did very much inquire after them. After a while, he traveled up farther towards the Dales in Yorkshire, as Wensdale and Sedbergh. Among the hills, dales, and mountains, he came on and convinced many of the eternal truth.

In the year 1652, it pleased the Lord to draw him towards us. He came on from Sedbergh and so to Westmorland, as Firbank Chapel, where John Blaykling came with him—so on to Preston, to Grayrigg, Kendal, Underbarrow, Poobank, Cartmel, and Staveley, and so on to Swarthmoor, my dwelling house, whither he brought the blessed tidings of the Everlasting Gospel, which I and many hundreds in these parts have cause to praise the Lord for. My then husband, Thomas Fell, was not at home at that time, but gone the Welsh Circuit, being one of the judges of the Assizes. Our house being a place open to entertain ministers and religious people at, one of George Fox's friends brought him hither, where he stayed all night. The next day, being a lecture, or a fastday, he went to Ulverston steeple house, but came not in, till people were gathered. I and my children had been a long time there before. When they were singing before the sermon, he came in. When they had done singing, he stood up upon a seat or form and desired that he might have liberty to speak. He that was in the pulpit said he might. The first words that he spoke were as follows: "He is not a Jew, that is one outward; neither is that circumcision, which is outward; that is circumcision, which is of the heart." He went on and said how Christ was the light of the world, and lights every man that comes into the world, and that by this light they might be gathered to God, etc. I stood up in my pew. I wondered at his doctrine, for I had never heard such before. Then he went on, and opened the scriptures, and said: The scriptures were the prophets' words, and Christ's and the Apostles' words, and what, as they spoke, they enjoyed and possessed, and had it from the Lord. [He] said, then what had any to do with the scriptures, but as they came to the Spirit that gave them forth. "You will say, Christ says this, and the apostles say this, but what can you say? Are you a child of light and have walked in the light? What you speak, is it inwardly from God?"

This opened me so, that it cut me to the heart. Then I saw clearly, we were all wrong. So I sat me down in my pew again, and cried bitterly. I cried in my spirit to the Lord, "We are all thieves, we are all thieves. We have taken the scriptures in words, and know nothing of them in ourselves." So that served me, that I cannot well tell what he spoke afterwards, but he went on declaring against the false prophets, priests, and deceivers of the people.

There was one John Sawrey, a Justice of the Peace and a professor, that bid the church warden, "Take him away." He laid his hands on him several times, took them off again, and let him alone. Then after a while, he gave over and came to our house again that night. He spoke in the family among the servants and they were all generally convinced, [such] as William Caton, Thomas Salthouse, Mary Askew, Anne Clayton, and several other servants. I was stricken into such a sadness, I knew not what to do, my husband being from home. I saw it was the truth. I could not deny it. I did, as the apostle said. I received the truth in the love of it. It was opened to me so clear that I had never a tittle in my heart against it, but I desired the Lord that I might be kept in it. Then I desired no greater portion.

He went on to Dalton, Aldingham, Dendron, and Rampside chapels, and steeple houses, and places several up and down. The people followed him mightily, abundant were convinced, and saw that which he spoke was truth. But the priests were all in a rage. About two weeks after, James Nayler and Richard Farnsworth followed him, inquired him out till they came to Swarthmoor, and there stayed a while with me at our house, and did me much good, for I was under great heaviness and judgment. The power of the Lord entered upon me, within about two weeks, that he came. About three weeks end, my husband came home. Many were in a mighty rage. A deal of the captains and great ones of the country went to meet my then husband, as he was coming home, and informed him that a great disaster was befallen among his family, that they were witches, that they had taken us out of our religion, that he might either set them away, or all the country would be undone. But no weapons formed against the Lord shall prosper, as you may see hereafter.

So my husband came home greatly offended. And any may think what a condition I was like to be in, that either I might displease my husband, or offend God, for he was very much troubled with us all in the house and family, they had so prepossessed him against us. But James Nayler and Richard Farnsworth were both then at our house. I desired them to come and speak to him. So they did, very moderately and wisely. He was at first displeased with them, but they told him, they came in love and good will to his house. After that he had heard them speak a while, he was better satisfied. They offered, as if they would go away, but I desired them to stay and not to go away yet, "for George Fox will come this evening." I would have had my husband to have heard them all and satisfied him farther about them, because they had so prepossessed him against them of such dangerous, fearful things in his coming first home. Then was he pretty moderate and quiet. His dinner being ready, he went to it. I went in and sat me down by him. While I was sitting, the power of the Lord seized upon me. He was stricken with amazement, and knew not what to think, but was quiet and still. The children were all quiet and still, grown sober, and could not play on their music, that they were learning. All these things made him quiet and still.

Then at night George Fox came. After supper my husband was sitting in the parlor. I asked him, if George Fox might come in? He said, "Yes." So George came in without any compliment, walked into the room, and began to speak presently. The family, James Nayler, and Richard Farnsworth came all in. He spoke very excellently, as ever I heard him, and opened Christ and the apostles' practices, which they were in, in their day. He opened the night of apostasy since the apostles' days, laid open the priests and their practices in the apostasy—that if all in England had been there, I thought, they could not have denied the truth of those things. So my husband came to see clearly the truth of what he spoke, was very quiet that night, said no more, and went to bed.

Next morning came Lampitt, priest of Ulverston, got my husband into the garden, and spoke much to him there. But my husband had seen so much the night before, that the priest got little entrance upon him. When the priest Lampitt was come into the house, George spoke sharply to him and asked him when God spoke to him, called him to go, and preach to the people? But after a while, the priest went away. This was on a sixth day, 1652.

At our house, diverse Friends were speaking one to another, how there were several convinced here a ways. We could not tell where to get a Meeting. My husband also being present, he overheard, and said of his own accord, "You may meet here, if you will." That was the first Meeting we had, that he offered of his own accord. Then notice was given that day and the next to Friends. There was a good large Meeting the first day, which was the first Meeting that was at Swarthmoor, and so continued there a Meeting from 1652 to 1690. My husband went that day to the steeple house, none with him, but his clerk and his groom, that rode with him. The priest and people were all fearfully troubled, but praised be the Lord, they never got their wills upon us to this day.

After a few weeks, George went to Ulverston steeple house again and the said Justice Sawrey, with others, set the rude rabble upon him. They beat him so that he fell down as in a swoon and was sore bruised and blackened in his body, on his head and arms. Then my husband was not at home, but when he came home, he was displeased that they should do so and spoke to Justice Sawrey, and said it was against the law to make riots. After that he [Fox] was sore beat and stoned at Walney, till he fell down. Also at Dalton was he sore beat and abused, so that he had very hard usage in diverse places in these parts. Then when a Meeting was settled here, he went again into Westmorland and settled Meetings there. There was a great convincement. Abundance of brave ministers came out there-ways, [such] as John Camm, John Audland, Francis Howgill, Edward Burrough, Miles Halhead, and John Blaykling with diverse others. He also went over Sands to Lancaster, Yealand, and Kellet, where Robert Widders, Richard Hubberthorne, and John Lawson, with many others, were convinced. About that time he was in those parts, many priests and professors rose up, and falsely accused him for blasphemy, did endeavor to take away his life, and got people to swear at a sessions at Lancaster, that he had spoken blasphemy. But my then husband and Colonel West, having had some sight and knowledge of the truth, withstood the two persecuting Justices, John Sawrey and Thompson, brought him off, and cleared him, for indeed he was innocent. After the sessions, there was a great Meeting in the town of Lancaster. Many townspeople came in and many were convinced. Thus he was up and down about Lancaster, Yealand, Westmorland, and some parts of Yorkshire and our parts above one year, in which time there were above twenty and four ministers brought forth, that were ready to go with their testimony of the eternal truth unto the world. Soon after, Francis Howgill and John Camm went to speak to Oliver Cromwell.

In the year 1653, George's drawings were into Cumberland by Millom, Lampley, Embleton and Brigham, Pardsley and Cockermouth, where at or near Embleton he had a dispute with some priests, [such] as Larkham and Benson, but chiefly with John Wilkinson, a preacher at Embleton and Brigham, who after was convinced, owned the truth, and was a serviceable minister both in England, Ireland, and Scotland. Then he [Fox] went to Coldbeck and several places, till he came to Carlisle, and went to their steeple house. They beat and abused him, had him before the magistrates who examined him, and put him in prison there in the common gaol among the thieves. At the Assizes, one Anthony Pearson—who had been a Justice of Peace and was convinced at Appleby (when he was upon the bench) by James Nayler and Francis Howgill, who were then prisoners there and brought before him—spoke to the Justices at Carlisle (he being acquainted with them, having married his wife out of Cumberland) and after a while they released him. After, he went into several parts in Cumberland and many were convinced and owned the truth. He gathered and settled meetings there among them, and up and down in several parts there in the North.

In the year 1654,[3] he went southward to his own country of Leicestershire, visiting Friends. Then Colonel Hacker sent him to Oliver Cromwell. After his being kept prisoner a while, he was brought before Oliver and was released. Then he stayed a while, visiting Friends in London and the Meetings therein, and so passed westward to Bristol, visited Friends there, and after went into Cornwall, where they put him in prison at Launceston, and one Edward Pyott with him, where he had a bad, long imprisonment. When he was released, he passed into many parts in that county of Cornwall and settled Meetings there. Then he traveled through many counties, visiting Friends and settling Meetings all along, so came into the North, to Swarthmoor and to Cumberland.

For Scotland, he passed in the year 1657 and there went with him Robert Widders, James Lancaster, John Grave, and others. He traveled through many places in that nation, [such] as Douglas, Heads, Hambleton, Glasgow, and to Edinburgh, where they took him, carried him before General Monk and the Council, examined him, and asked him his business in that nation. [Fox] answered he came to visit the seed of God. After they had threatened him and charged him to depart their nation of Scotland, they let him go. Then he went to Linlithgow, Stirling, Johnstons, and many places, visiting the people, and several were convinced. After he had stayed a pretty while and settled some Meetings, he returned into Northumberland and into Bishoprick of Durham, visiting Friends and settling Meetings as he went, and then returned back again to Swarthmoor, stayed among Friends a while, and so returned South again. In 1658, Judge Fell died.

In 1660, he [Fox] came out of the South into the North, had a great General Meeting about Balby in Yorkshire, and so came on visiting Friends in many places, till he came to Swarthmoor again. King Charles then being come in, the Justices sent out warrants, took him at Swarthmoor, charging him in their warrants that he drew away the King's liege people to the endangering and imbruing the nation in blood, and sent him prisoner to Lancaster Castle. I having a great family and he being taken in my house, I was moved of the Lord to go to the King at Whitehall and took with me a declaration and an information of our principles.[4] A long time and much ado I had to get to him. But at last, when I got to him, I told him, if he [Fox] was guilty of those things, I was guilty, for he was taken in my house. I gave him the paper of our principles and desired that he would set him at liberty, as he had promised, "that none should suffer for tender consciences." We were of tender consciences and desired nothing, but the liberty of our consciences. Then with much ado, after he had been kept prisoner near half a year at Lancaster, we got a *Habeas Corpus* and removed him to the King's Bench, where he was released. Then would I gladly have come home to my great family, but was bound in my spirit and could not have freedom to get away for a whole year. The King promised me several times that we should have our liberty. Then the [Fifth] Monarchy Men rose and then came the great and general imprisonment of Friends the nation through. So could I not have freedom nor liberty to come home, till we had got a General Proclamation for all our Friends' liberty. Then I had freedom and peace to come home.

In 1664, he [Fox] came North again and to Swarthmoor. Then they sent out warrants, took him again, had him to Holcross, before the Justices, tendered him the Oath of Allegiance, and sent him prisoner to Lancaster Castle. About a month after, the Justices sent for me also out of my house, tendered me the Oath, and sent me prisoner to Lancaster. The next Assizes, they tendered the Oath of Allegiance and Supremacy to us again both and praemunired me, but they missed the date and other things in his indictment. So it was quashed, but they tendered him the Oath again and kept him prisoner a year and a half at Lancaster Castle. Then they sent him to Scarborough Castle in Yorkshire, where they kept him prisoner close under the soldiers much of a year and a half, so that a Friend could scarcely have spoken to him. Yet after that it pleased the Lord, that he was released. I continued in prison and a prisoner four years at that time. An order was procured from the Council, whereby I was set at liberty. In that time, I went down into Cornwall with my son and daughter Lower, and came back by London to the Yearly Meeting. There I met with him [Fox] again. Then he told me, the time was drawing on towards our marriage, but he might first go into Ireland. A little before this time was he prisoner in his own country of Leicester for a while, and then released. So, into Ireland he went. I went into Kent and Sussex and came back to London again. Afterward, I went to the West, toward Bristol in 1669 and there I stayed, till he came over from Ireland. Then it was eleven years after my former husband's decease. In Ireland, he had had a great service for the Lord and his eternal truth, among Friends and many people there, but escaped many dangers and times of being taken prisoner, they having laid in wait aforehand for him in many places. Then he being returned, at Bristol, he declared his intentions of marriage. There also was our marriage solemnized. Then, within ten days after, I came homewards. My husband stayed up and down in the countries among Friends visiting them.

Soon after I came home, there came another order from the Council to cast me into prison again. The Sheriff of Lancashire sent his bailiff, pulled me out of my own house, and had me prisoner to Lancaster Castle (upon the old Praemunire), where I continued a whole year. Most part of all that time was I sick and weakly. Also my husband was weak and sickly at that time. Then after a while he recovered, went about to get me out of prison, and a discharge at least was got under the Great Seal. So I was set at liberty. Then I was to go up to London again, for my husband was intending for America. He was full two years away, before he came back into England. Then he arrived at Bristol, and came to London. He intended to have come to the middle of the nation with me. But when we came into some parts of Worcestershire, they got their information of him, and one Justice Parker by his warrant sent him and my son Lower to Worcester Gaol. The Justices there rendered him of Oath and praemunired him, but released my son Lower, who stayed with him most of the time he was prisoner there.

After some time he fell sick in a long, lingering sickness, and many times was very ill, so they wrote to me from London, that if I would see him alive, I might go to him, which accordingly I did. After I had tarried seventeen weeks with him at Worcester and no discharge like to be obtained for him, I went up to London and wrote to the King an account of his long imprisonment, how he was taken in his travel homewards, how he was weak and sick and not likely to live, if they kept him long there. I went with it to Whitehall myself. I met with the King and gave him my paper. He said I must go to the Lord Chancellor. He could do nothing in it. Then I wrote also to the Lord Chancellor, went to his house, gave him my paper, and spoke to him, that the King had left it wholly to him—and if he did not take pity and release him out of that prison, I feared he would end his days there. The Lord Chancellor Finch was a very tender man and spoke to the judge, who gave out a Habeas Corpus presently. When we got it, we sent it down to Worcester. They would not part with him at first, but said he was praemunired and was not to go out on that manner. Then we were forced to go to Judge North and to the Attorney General. We got another order, sent down from them, and with much ado, great labour and industry of William Meade and other Friends, we got him up to London, where he appeared in Westminster Hall at the King's Bench, before Judge Hale, who was a very honest, tender man. He knew they had imprisoned him but in envy. So that which they had against him was read. Our counsel pleaded "that he was taken up in his travel and journey." There was but a little said, till he was quitted. This was the last prison that he was in, being freed by the Court of the King's Bench.

When he was at liberty, he recovered again. Then I was very desirous to go home with him, which we did. This was the first time that he came to Swarthmoor after we were married. So he stayed here much of two years, then [he] went to London again to the Yearly Meeting, and after a while went into Holland and some parts of Germany, where he stayed a pretty while, then returned to London again at the next Yearly Meeting. After he had stayed a while in and about London, he came into the North to Swarthmoor again and stayed that time nigh two years. Then he grew weakly, being troubled with pains and aches, having had many sore and long travels, beatings, and hard imprisonments. But after some time he rode to York, so passed on through Nottinghamshire and several counties, visiting Friends, till he came to London to the Yearly Meeting, stayed there and thereaways, till he finished his course and laid down his head in peace.

Though the Lord had provided an outward habitation for him, yet he was not willing to stay at it, because it was so remote and far from London, where his service most lay. My concern for God and His holy, eternal truth was then in the North, where God had placed and set me, and likewise for the ordering and governing of my children and family, so that we were very willing both of us, to live apart some years upon God's account and

His truth's service, and to deny ourselves of that comfort which we might have had in being together, for the sake and service of the Lord and His truth. If any took occasion, or judged hard of us because of that, the Lord will judge them, for we were innocent. For my own part, I was willing to make many long journeys, for taking away all occasion for evil thoughts. Though I lived two-hundred miles from London, yet have I been nine times there, upon the Lord and His truth's account. Of all the times that I was at London, this last time was most comfortable, that the Lord was pleased to give me strength and ability to travel that great journey, being seventy-six years of age, to see my dear husband, who was better in health and strength than many times I had seen him before. I look upon that, that the Lord's special hand was in it, that I should go then, for he lived but about half a year after I left him, which makes me admire the wisdom and goodness of God in ordering my journey at that time.

Now he has finished his course and his testimony and is entered into his eternal rest and felicity. I trust in the same powerful God, that His holy arm and power will carry me through whatever He has yet for me to do, that He will be my strength and support and the bearer up of my head unto the end and in the end. I know His faithfulness and goodness. I have experienced of His love, to whom be glory and powerful dominion forever. Amen.

Margaret Fell

Some of the Sayings of Margaret Fox in the Time of Her Sickness, A Little Before Her Departure Out of This World

"Come, come, pray let us join the Lord, and be of one spirit; join to the eternal God and be of one spirit."

Her daughter expressing what a blessed mother she had been to her children and whole posterity, she answered very sweetly, "Cleave to me, and you will not do wrong, for I am joined to the Lord."

And again, to her grandson, "Dear John, dear John, stand for God, stand for God," repeating those words to him several times, and said, "I have nothing that troubles me."

And another time, her daughter expressing her sorrow to part with her and desire that her life might be spared, she said, she did not know but the Lord might grant it, but said, "His will be done."

Again, her daughter expressing our intentions to educate her grandson, our son, according to her mind and desire, she said, "All that I desire for him is that he may be faithful."

At another time, she said, "Oh! My sweet Lord, into your holy bosom do I commit myself freely, not desiring to live in this troublesome, painful world. It is all nothing to me: for my Maker is my husband."

At another time, she said, "Come Lord Jesus, I am freely given up to your will."

At another time, "I have a clear conscience."

An ancient Friend, Thomas Dockrey, coming to see her, said to her, "Dear heart, how do you find yourself?" She answered, "Very weak of body, but alive to God."

Again, she said, "I freely forgive all people upon the face of the whole earth, for any wrong done to me, as freely as I desire to be forgiven."

She said to her grandson, "John, the Lord loves you, and will love you for my sake, and my prayers and tears that I have put up to Him for you many times."

And seeing us sorrowful, she said, "Be quiet, for I am as comfortable, and well in my spirit, as ever I was."

And a little before she parted, she called Rachel, saying, "Take me in your arms," and then said, "I am in peace."

STUDY GUIDE

An Introductory Note

As a young instructor thirty years ago, I paired with an older colleague and mentor who proved to be a master teacher with great wisdom and experience. One day, however, he confessed that as a beginning teacher, he had his mishaps and miscarriages. Straight out of college, he'd been hired to teach at a well known boys' school. At the end of the year, he met with his supervisor to assess whether he should receive a contract for a second year.

"Before we render any decision on whether to offer you a contract renewal for next year," the supervisor observed, "I need the answer to one question: Which do you really want to do, teach boys or teach English?"

My colleague returned, without a moment's hesitation, "I want to teach English."

"Then," said the supervisor, "you'll need to find a job elsewhere, for our mission here is to teach boys."

What does this little anecdote have to do with the present Study Guide? Just this: In creating the guide I had to ask myself whether I wanted to create the usual guide with its simple goal of assisting and directing the study of its subject—in this case the life, faith, ministry, and works of Margaret Fell Fox—or did I wish to offer a guide that would assist twenty-first century Quaker Christians in comparing their faith and practice with our first Friends, with the aims of:

+ helping to establish Friends to the true and firm foundation of our living Lord;
+ deepening our understanding of what is central and unique about our Quaker Christian faith; and
+ realizing the full witness we are called to in our day.

Our early Friends did not *think* or *believe* they had found the true and firm foundation, they *knew* they had found it by their experience of their Lord Jesus Christ's presence and power in their lives. He gave them the power to break the bonds of sin in this life and to do His will. The One our first Friends experienced was the same living Lord with the same extraordinary power that the early Christian church knew.

Today too many Quakers of all persuasions have lost sight of what was central and unique about our Quaker Christian faith and have an extremely difficult time defining how they are different than various other Christian and non-Christian groups. Those Friends who follow programmed worship and who have accepted a Methodist or Congregational polity, might well ask, "Why not take the final step and embrace Methodism or Congregationalism, for those bodies 'do it better' and have far more resources?" Likewise, those Friends who espouse a non-programmed form of worship and liberal activism and eschew a Christian identification might well ask, "Why not take the final step and embrace the Unitarian-Universalists or one of the religions they often mention and espouse in their discussions and literature?" And those who label themselves Evangelical might well ask, "Why be Quakers, when so many Evangelical congregations seem far more dynamic and resourced and able to give far more active leadership and support?"

If the only justifications Meetings can embrace as to why, at the present time, they carry the name *Quaker* or *Friend* are:

+ we've always been Quakers;
+ this is where I grew up;
+ this is my family's church and always has been; or
+ we don't know, we just are,

the Great Physician Christ Jesus will rightly conclude they are in dire need of a heart transplant.

There is no substantial reason to embrace Quakerism if there is nothing to differentiate it from other groups and churches. However, if our original Quaker faith—the central and often neglected faith, witness, and power of early Christianity—challenges us with essential Christianity, the power, presence, and leading of Jesus Christ our Lord and the witness He commands us to make, then that Quaker faith is central and essential to our lives.

This is what Margaret Fell is saying: Here is essential Christianity. Here is the living faith that brought me from the moribund churches of my time, the confused and chaotic claims of competing religions that simply confused people more, the dead witness of groups that professed to be Christian, but whose actions put the lie to their high claims: angry, violent, subversive actions; fraudulent claims and political plotting; jangling and schismatic tendencies.

Some things have changed little since Fell's time. Yes, we've far more sophisticated technology, but also even greater confusion reigns than in Fell's time—both in the world and in the churches—as to the nature of Christianity and to what Christians should witness. Margaret Fell, herself, testifies she spent years trying to be a good Christian, but with no inward or outward confirmation that she had found what she sought until she heard the Good News and met the Truth in Christ Jesus.

The question today is: do we possess what we profess? Or have we got the words of scripture, but not the power of the living Word, Jesus Christ our Lord? If the latter, we must grieve with Fell, who cried, "We are all thieves! We are all thieves! We have got the words without the power." But, like Fell, we can come into, and grow in, possession by coming into clarity concerning the Kingdom of our Lord, His will for us, and how we must live.

This is the goal of the studies on which we are about to embark. May you be blessed in them.

CHAPTER 1

A True Testimony from the People of God...
How Does the Witness of Our Lives Measure Up?

Introduction

How do we measure our faith, ourselves, our words and actions, as Quaker Christians in the twenty-first century? Do we use the latest television news reports concerning strange and arcane happenings among Christians, the media's loud reports of priestly and pastoral sins and abuses, and those brief and unexamined pronouncements by obscure "authorities" on "new discoveries" about Christian origins? Do we apply what we've been taught by others (either positively or negatively) about the scriptures and what it means to "be Christian"? Do we profess to be followers of Christ and God's people because that's what our family, friends, and church leaders have told us we've always been, and are? *Or are we the People of God, because we have met Christ Jesus, our living Lord, and He has gathered us together and leads us as our shepherd, king, priest, prophet, bishop, orderer, and savior?*

In coming to a firm and well founded answer, Margaret Fell exhorts us to use our Lord's own measuring rod—the commandments, doctrines, fellowship, and spiritual fruits that God's true people embrace, live by, and show forth. Margaret Fell claims in her pamphlet, *A True Testimony from the People of God,* that the experience, doctrines, and witness of Friends are identical in both power and spirit with those of the prophets, Christ Jesus, and His apostles. Thus, the workings and fruits of the spirit in the lives of the prophets, Jesus Christ, and His apostles served as the measuring rod and check for Fell and our first Friends, both in their own lives and as they were confronted by the experiences, doctrines, challenges, and claims of others—others many of whom claimed to be Christian but did not live like true Christians, and some espoused no faith at all.

Contrary to some modern claims that people can and should believe anything they want, because beliefs have no consequences, the truth is: what we believe has momentous consequences, profound consequences, for remarkable good or terrible evil. A host of creeds like Nazism and Communism, and hundreds of social engineering proposals, all claim that their actions will bring a new age of "progress," harmony, justice, and happiness. In attempting to improve the human condition, they have brought deeper darkness upon humanity, injustice on a staggering scale, chaos, and atrocities. Even those who possess the scriptures and claim to be in the "Christian tradition" have been dramatically guilty of falling short of their Lord's will. Regrettably, Fell's observation concerning many Christians in her own time, still appears true today:

> They, having their words and writings upon record, do make these a sufficient testimony for them of their knowledge and worship of God, and so preach, teach, take texts out of these words, add thereunto their own inventions, and so feed poor ignorant people with these.

The earliest Quaker Christian generations laid down the spiritual measuring rod of their Lord. He revealed both His loving presence and His power to them and empowered them faithfully to do His will. That faithfulness bore dramatic spiritual fruits, strong evidence of Christ Jesus' presence among them. Yet, these same Friends faced a similar situation to ours today: a plethora of competing "spiritualities," philosophies, sects, and cults jockeying for their attention and new adherents.

Exercise

The following exercise is designed to help us lay down that same spiritual measuring rod that our first Friends used. The goal of the exercise is to help us toward clarity on the nature and demands of our faith and how those demands are different from that to which both the world and many who profess to be Christian call us.

The first step of this exercise is to make sure we understand the essential Quaker witness and how it is different from what many groups profess. We must understand the marks of what it means to be a true Christian before we can measure. If we have no clarity on what we are looking at, we will simply go from confusion to chaos.

1. The Apostasy (the failure of many in Christendom to follow Christ)

    Read aloud the early Quaker definition of the apostasy on pages 25-28. Write down what it is and what evidence our first Friends used to confirm its existence and presence in their time.

    Jot down and discuss with others in your group the present day evidence you believe suggests that the apostasy is still very much with us, in spite of all the talk about ecumenism, Christian cooperation, dialogue, progress, and liberalization.

    If time permits, return to the scriptures. There one can find evidence from Genesis through the Revelation that the apostasy has been with us from the beginning. To begin your work, consider Israel's unfaithfulness to God's first covenant, the challenges of the prophets to the "religious" leaders of their day, Jesus' confrontation of the Pharisees and Sadducees. Share your examples with others.

2. Immediate Revelation

    Carefully define it and consider thoughtfully the following admonition concerning immediate and continuing revelation: Immediate revelation, when it appears in the Christian tradition, does not mean that our Lord is giving a new revelation that supersedes older revelations. Both Catholics and Quakers traditionally have understood that our Lord is not changeable so as to forbid a thing (like war or adultery) and then later lead us unto it. A supposed immediate revelation that cuts against earlier revelations is a major danger signal that we are going astray and that we will soon be lost in uncharted, unchecked, uncheckable territory. If we believe that God is regularly changing and superseding His own revelations, the whole of Christianity is "up for grabs" and we'll end up with a brew of our own brain-battered notions, politics, and desires.

3. What is true worship?

4. What is the difference between ministers of the world and ministers of God and His Spirit?

5. What are the consequences that develop from the worship of God in Spirit and in Truth?

    a. Coming into the firm fellowship and foundation of the Gospel

b. Experiencing the ministrations of the Spirit

c. Being strengthened in the Spirit by keeping the unity in the Spirit and body of peace

d. Coming to experience the fullness of God's love and the cleansing of the conscience

e. Bringing forth the fruits of the Spirit: love, gentleness, fairness, temperateness, etc. (see Galatians 5:22).

When you're through with your analysis and group discussion, consider how coming to know and obey the living Christ will call forth significant changes in our lives. Consider Mary Poplin's experience:

> As the fog was lifted from my mind, I began to see how the fundamental principles of life with Christ were so the opposite of my own automatic ways of thinking, being, and reacting. I realized that to live a Christian life, I would have to live it upside-down or inside-out from all I have known before.

CHAPTER 2

A Declaration of Quaker Principles and Practice...
We Wear the Name, But Do We Bear It?

Introduction

Margaret Fell's declaration to the King and both Houses of Parliament brings today's Quakers face-to-face with the question of who they are, or aren't. *We Are the People of God Called Quakers...* declared *who* Friends were in the seventeenth century, *what* they stood for, and *why* they stood for it.

They were *the people of God*, not merely individuals who had a personal relationship with Him. They were frankly and forthrightly Christian, not *only* in word, but very distinctly in deed. Their lives testified to the presence of Jesus Christ within them, because their actions ran so directly contrary to the prevailing and supposed Christian culture of their time. When other groups bowed and scraped to their "betters," Quakers refused, testifying to the equality of all before God. When various groups, like the Anglicans and the Presbyterians, lied and dissembled about their activities during periods when their worship was out-of-favor and outlawed, Friends unflinchingly and openly met for worship, acted and spoke truthfully, and went to prison for their faithfulness. When government troops or rioters broke up Friends' Meetings for Worship with threats, violence, and physical abuse, Quakers refused to return violence for violence, testifying that they fought only with spiritual weapons, combating deceit with Truth, identifying their enemies' violence and hatred as inimical to the commands of Jesus Christ.

Exercise

Step One: Developing Our Own Declaration

1. First, if your group is large, break up into small groups of five to eight. Appoint a scribe to take notes on the group's deliberations, and a facilitator, whose chief purpose will be to keep the group on task.

2. The task is to develop a modern declaration of who we are as today's people called Quakers.

3. The group(s) should focus on what our actions say about who we are as much as on our beliefs, recognizing that Quakers have traditionally emphasized that their faith is more than talk. So we talk-the-talk, but do we walk-the-walk? Do our actions contradict our profession of who we are or bear witness that we truly live and walk according to our Lord's will?

4. If the number involved in the exercise is large, bring everyone together after the small groups have worked for twenty minutes to a half-hour on their task.

   a. Have scribes report on each small group's findings.

   b. Have someone capture the essence of each report on a black or white board, or a newsprint easel.

   c. Given that the size of a large group activity takes greater time to address its task than a small group, the large group may want to schedule the next task for the next meeting of the full group, rather than immediately continuing on at this point.

5.   However, if the group is small, Friends can move directly to the next step below.

Step Two: Assessing Our Declaration

Our Lord made it clear to us many times during His ministry that words alone are not enough, that our life in Him must blossom and bring forth clear, recognizable, and distinct fruits. Read Matthew 5:44-48 and/or consider Matthew 7:21-23:

> Not everyone who says to me, "Lord, Lord," will enter the kingdom of heaven, but only the one who does the will of my Father in heaven. On that day many will say to me, "Lord, Lord, did we not prophesy in your name, and cast out demons in your name, and do many deeds of power in your name?" Then I will declare to them, "I never knew you; go away from me, you evil doers."

Likewise, Christ's apostles emphasize that our Lord's presence produces visible and tangible works. Consider 1 Corinthians 13:1-3, Galatians 5:16-26, and James 1:19-27.

Now compare and contrast your group's declaration with Fell's:

+   On what do they differ?
+   Where are they alike?
+   What has been left out of today's declaration?
+   Review the teaching and commandments of our Lord: Does today's declaration ignore or compromise the life to which He calls us?

Chapter 3

Women's Speaking Justified...
What We Have to Open to the Rest of Christendom

Introduction

Women's Speaking Justified, Proved, and Allowed... is as relevant and fresh in our time as it was when Margaret Fell wrote it over 350 years ago. Many Evangelical denominations still question women's role in church government, some refuse to ordain women, and others declare women must keep silent. The Orthodox and Roman Catholic churches continue to cite scriptures and tradition as reasons for not ordaining women to the priesthood, even though the record of scripture does not bear out such a stricture (as Fell so effectively demonstrates) and ancient tradition is less than completely supportive of their position.

Exercise

We have had it drummed into us so often that women should "keep silent" in church, that when we hear the opposite, it sounds like a radical and suspect departure. Moreover, Paul's statements in 1 Corinthians and 1 Timothy, that women be submissive to their husbands, seems to be, at first glance, his teaching to married Christians.

However, Margaret Fell has presented so many scriptures concerning Paul's acceptance of women's ministry and speaking in church that she definitely has the weight of evidence on her side for an understanding. The key point here hinges on whether the speaker is a New Creation—a New Woman in Christ Jesus—or a soul still in the Fall and betraying the fruits of that Fall.

1. Identify and discuss further evidence in the Gospels and Paul's letters that support Margaret Fell's position.

2. Given that fallen humanity so misinterprets and misunderstands Paul's concern on women in the Fall keeping silent in church, it is useful to examine a second misinterpretation—that women must be submissive to their husbands. Paul's statements in 1 Corinthians 14:26f and 1 Timothy 2:11f have been exploited by all manner of misanthropes and misogynists to justify their domination, and even abuse, of women. However, when we look at the totality of Paul's description of marriage, we find something quite different. (Read the appendix material before going further.)

If we are truly New Creatures in Christ Jesus, our relationship with our spouse is transformed and transfigured. The old relationship, based too often on patriarchy and domination, gives way to a new relationship of servant-hood, of loving service to one another. We become helpmates. When one reads the entirety of Paul's comments on marriage, one will find that our Lord and His love cancels man's dominion and woman's submission, roles characteristic of our fallen state but not of our redemption.

1. Read together Paul's comments in 1 Corinthians 7, Ephesians 5:21-33, and Colossians 3:1-20. Discuss the nature of the marriage relationship when we are in a fallen state, and what changes or what fruits should appear when we begin to grow into New Men and Women.

2. Paul recognizes that not all marriages are between two people who have both embraced Christ Jesus as their Lord, Savior, and leader. Yet, this does not release us who are New Creatures from our responsibilities and commitments to our spouses—or our love. Those who are growing as God's New Creatures must still show forth Christ's presence and His love to the unbelieving spouse. Discuss the special problems faced by such marriages and discuss how Christ's love in us for our spouse should address such problems.

3. As a result of the Fall, scripture tells us that God put "enmity between" the serpent and the woman. Think of, and share, instances when you have witnessed this "enmity" between serpent and woman.

Chapter 4

Some Ranters' Principles Answered
Ranters of Our Own Day

Introduction

When I first came across those individuals called the Ranters who infested England and made life difficult for our first Friends in the seventeenth century, I murmured to myself: "I *know* these people!" Of course, they're not called Ranters today—in fact the term "Ranters" is not even in the computer dictionary program I'm using while I write this introduction.

Yet, it is extremely important to understand today what the Ranters were—and still are—for with the collapse in the Western world of religious and social value systems over the last forty years, Ranterism has not only reappeared (some would say it never really disappeared, but is simply more evident in certain ages like our own), but reappeared with a vengeance. The primary reason I included Margaret Fell's *Some Ranters' Principles Answered* was not from a love of the arcane and anachronistic, but because Ranterism is rampant today. Sharpening our ability to identify it and address it is imperative for both our spiritual and social health.

Exercise

1. First, we must be clear on the species of thinking and behavior which we are examining. Behavior follows belief just as particular kinds of soil allow certain kinds of plants to appear and thrive. What we believe does bear consequences.

Thus, it is important that we first ground ourselves by studying the following list of characteristic Ranter ideas and behaviors:

A. Antinomian ("against law"),
B. Directed toward the destruction of moral law in the interest of individual freedom,
C. Espouse moral relativism,
D. Emphasize subjectivity and individualism over order and community,
E. Deny subjection to any law other than the individual desire and caprice,
F. Forward and extravagant in their claims to spiritual insight,
G. Rampant with wild imaginings, lack of spiritual seriousness, and often commonsense decorum,
H. Negative behaviors like lying, cheating, adultery, drunkenness, drug use—which are often used to justify plotting, murder, and treason.

2. Second, in preparation for a group discussion, identify some modern instances of Ranter thinking and behavior. Feel free to range over the entire last century. You might discuss one or more of the following questions in your group:

A. Did Communism and Nazism espouse certain antinomian attitudes to forward their revolutions?
B. Have some theologians and clergy fallen into Ranterism by not challenging moral relativism?
C. Have school programs that suggest instances when behaviors like lying, cheating, stealing, adultery, and drug use might be justified actually be moving their students toward Ranter thinking and behavior?

D. Is the rampant wild imagining, lack of spiritual seriousness, and absence of commonsense decorum in the media and in the cinema reflective of rampant Ranter tendencies among the elite in our Western societies?

3. Third, identify the answer our first Friends gave and lived against Ranterism in their day.

4. Finally, discuss what such an answer and witness is required of us in the face of such a tsunami of Ranterism in our own time.

Chapter 5

Margaret Fell Fox in Her Own Words
Coping with the Burdens of Ministry, Then and Now

Introduction

The group of Margaret Fell's autobiographical documents and writings are, of course, of interest in themselves, well beyond their usefulness as historical documents. They can and do give us inspiring insights into the heart and thinking of one who is among the greatest of the early women ministers of her time. It is clear from early Quaker history that our Lord raised Margaret Fell to be one of the indispensable leaders and administrators in the rise and support of His people in the seventeenth century.

Exercise

Two Quaker Friends of mine married a number of years ago. They were in age similar to George Fox and Margaret Fell when those two early Quaker worthies married. In fact, like Margaret Fell, the bride had been widowed some years before, and like Fox, the groom was entering marriage for the first time. During the Meeting for Worship after the couple exchanged their vows, each rose to speak. The groom shocked those present, when he announced that he and his bride had to get married. He continued that this marriage was an "arranged marriage," further shocking the congregation. Then, in the stunned hush that followed these two announcements, he announced that they had to get married because it was arranged by our Lord, who had brought them together to strengthen their ministries to others. His bride, too, was moved to rise and preach before the Meeting ended.

Friends left awed, knowing that they had witnessed a marriage quite different from those our popular culture fosters. This was no couple brought together by "love at first sight." They had not recognized one another as their other half ("better half"). This was not a marriage founded on the shifting sands of emotion. It was a marriage formed by our Lord and the couple acted at His direction and in His will to strengthen His work and kingdom.

Explore the many differences such a marriage entails and contrast it to the popular concept of marriage in American culture today. How does putting our Lord's will first in marriage change our entire relationship with our spouse? How does it put such an intimate relationship on a true and firm foundation? Include in your discussion the many sacrifices the Fell/Fox marriage of ministries required of them over their lifetime.

APPENDICES

George Whitehead's Testimony[1] Concerning Our Beloved Ancient Friend Margaret Fell by her First Marriage, Margaret Fox by her Second

Her kind and early reception of the servants and ministers of Christ in his name and truth met with the reward of a blessed disciple, which she became, through God's great love, and gracious visitation.

Of a noble generous spirit, she was greatly serviceable to truth and Friends in her day, and effectually gained upon her first husband, Judge Fell, by her innocent and prudent conversation (according to 1 Pet. 3:1-2) whereby he became more Friendly[2] and kind to Friends in early days, and was instrumental to moderate the persecutions toward our Friends in Lancashire and those parts of the north of England.

She was very industrious in her solicitations and frequent applications to King Charles the Second, after the severe persecution and great imprisonments begun in the years 1661 and 1662, and earnestly endeavored to persuade him to put a stop to those persecutions and to relieve our Friends from those hardships which many were under in those times. She tenderly cleared her conscience in plainness to him,[3] and at last when she was clear, committed her endeavors and left the issue of all to the Lord, the righteous judge of all. In her great industry and endeavors for Friends' relief, she truly manifested her tender love to the heritage of God, sympathizing with the sufferers for his name's and truth's sake. The Lord helped and supported her in her great labors of love for his suffering Seed's sake.

She was preserved and continued in a good understanding and testimony for the blessed truth in life and doctrine, in the spirit of love, and of a sound mind, being zealous for the name of the Lord and his living truth, for which she also was a great sufferer.

She had a godly care upon her for the sober and virtuous education of her children and offspring.[4] The Lord blessed and answered her therein, in a good measure, and no doubt blessed them the more for her sake, as well as for their own salvation, for which she chiefly travailed in spirit and earnestly sought the Lord in their behalf, beyond all temporal blessings.

She retained a sincere and constant love to all faithful Friends and brethren to the end, which was a true evidence of her being passed from death to life, while here, and of her portion in eternal life and felicity in the heavenly kingdom, the inheritance of all the faithful in Christ Jesus: to whom be glory and dominion forever and ever.

London, the 23rd of the Second Month, 1709.
George Whitehead

Domination, Submission, and the New Creation
By T.H.S. Wallace

If you are in the Fall, you cannot and do not read the scriptures in the Spirit in which they were given. You will misread and misinterpret what you find there. Take, for instance, that famous exhortation, "Wives, submit to your husbands..." (Ephesians 5:22) and "a woman should learn in quietness and full submission. I do not permit a woman to teach or to have authority over a man; she must be silent" (1 Tim. 2:11-12). Because of the constant reiteration of these verses in both the worldly and the religious media, you'd think they were all Paul said on the subject. The male chauvinist rises up and cries, "Yes, woman! Down! Heel! Submit!" And the radical feminist cries back, "Never! I will never submit to ANY man!"

Reading the Scriptures in the Spirit

As Quaker Christians, we need to return to the practice of our earliest Friends in Christ, the practice of:

+ Reading scripture in the same Spirit in which it was written, letting Christ Jesus open its meaning to us.
+ Reading the scriptures honestly, not picking and choosing what gratifies our ego and ignoring the rest. Reading *honestly* means:
  o Reading the full context in which verses are set,
  o Taking what the entire passage is saying into account,
  o And how the entire passage fits into the entirety of, say, Paul's letters, Peter's letters, the Gospels— yea, the very totality of the scriptures.
+ Reading prayerfully, asking our Lord to reveal as He wills and at the time He wills the spiritual meaning of what is before us.

We have seen the devastating clarity that these practices brought to Margaret Fell's pamphlet on *Women's Speaking,* for her extensive review of the scriptural support for women speaking in church, when they are moved by Christ Jesus to do so, demolishes centuries of selective and slanted readings of scripture designed to reinforce humanity's fallen status, rather than build men and women up in the New Life into which they are brought by our Lord.

How We Have Read Paul Wrong

When we read the Pauline letters fully on the subject of husbands and wives, we will find the apostle puts a markedly different emphasis on the married state than we have traditionally been taught. Let us take, first, his letter to the Ephesians. Note that the passage does *not* begin with the admonition of "Wives, submit to your husbands..." This admonition is part of a longer exhortation to the Ephesians to:

> have nothing to do with the fruitless deeds of darkness, but rather expose them. For it is shameful even to mention what the disobedient [the Fallen] do in secret. But everything exposed by the light becomes visible, for it is light that makes everything visible. This is why it is said: "Wake up, O sleeper, rise from the dead, and Christ will shine on you."

Expositors rarely note that Paul admonishes, "Be very careful, then, how you live..." and before he mentions "Wives, submit...," his exhortation actually begins, "Submit to one another out of reverence for Christ," and Paul does not simply say, "submit to your husbands...," but "submit to your husbands *as to the Lord.*" Paul's letter to the Colossians says it a tad differently, "Wives, submit to your husbands, *as is fitting in the Lord,*" and follows this instruction immediately with one for husbands: "love your wives and do not be harsh with them."

What Paul Truly Meant by Submission

The emphasis in these passages is on far more than submission: it is first on our relationship with our Lord, as His New Creatures, that relationship recreating, informing, and changing our most intimate relationships with one another. Yes, Paul does immediately say that:

> the husband is the head of the wife as Christ is the head of the church, his body, of which he is the Savior. Now as the church submits to Christ, so also wives should submit to their husbands in everything.

But the question we should be asking is not, "How could Paul say such a thing!?" It should be, "How does Christ act as head of the church, His body?" And, "How are we to submit to Christ?"

To answer fully those two questions goes far beyond the scope of this little paper, but I can begin to open the answer and encourage those in Christ to continue His work in their own lives. How does Christ act as head of His body, the church? Is He harsh, dominating, violent, bitter, irritable, angry, wrathful, nasty, irrational, penurious? Obviously not! He suppers with us. He calls us His Friends. He leads us gently, compassionately, patiently. He is kind and loving, long suffering, steadfast.

And how are we to submit to Christ? Paul tell us, in Ephesians 5, "Be imitators of God, therefore, as dearly loved children, and live a life of love, just as Christ loved us and gave himself up for us as a fragrant offering and sacrifice to God." In Colossians 3:8-10, Paul tells us that, in Christ:

now you must rid yourselves of all such things as these: anger, rage, malice, slander, filthy language from your lips. Do not lie to each other, since you have taken off your old self with its practices and put on the new self, which is being renewed in knowledge in the image of its Creator. Here there is no Greek or Jew, circumcised or uncircumcised, barbarian, Scythian, slave or free [or *male or female*, as Paul will add in Galatians 3:26- 29], but Christ is all, and is in all.

A woman's submission to her husband is to be the same as her submission to Christ. And in submitting to Christ, her husband also thus submits himself *to her*, for that submission is to be "as to the Lord" and "as is fitting in the Lord."

Paul defines that submission in very clear terms in Colossians 3:12-14: "Therefore, as God's chosen people, holy and dearly loved, clothe yourselves with compassion, kindness, humility, gentleness, and patience. Bear with each other and forgive whatever grievances you may have against one another. Forgive as the Lord forgave you. And over all these virtues put on love, which finds them all together in perfect unity."

The "yes, but" old creature within us may, of course, retort, "but wait! This applies only to marriages between husbands and wives who have submitted themselves to their Lord! My husband or wife rejects faith in Christ Jesus. Doesn't this change everything?" Paul answers with a resounding, "No." An unbelieving spouse changes nothing, either in our relationship with Christ Jesus or in our marital relationship, if that spouse chooses to continue in marriage. Divorce is not an option for the believing spouse, though Paul recognizes the reality that the unbelieving spouse may choose to abandon the marriage. The believing spouse, though, has a special responsibility—to recognize and embrace the fact that his or her continued faithfulness may lead to the sanctification of the unbelieving spouse.

The Abolition of the Old Domination/Submission Relationship

The most important thing I realized years ago about Paul's teachings on our married life is that:

1. The old domination/submission relationship between men and women in the Fall is abolished, and
2. Paul's teachings, on wives submitting and husbands loving, actually in their effects cancel out the old domination/submission relationship.

The fullness of Paul's teachings here come home when we realize how they relate to his declaration in Galatians, that we:

> are all sons of God through faith in Christ Jesus, for all of you who were baptized into Christ have clothed yourselves with Christ. There is neither Jew nor Greek, slave nor free, male nor female, for you are all one in Christ Jesus. If you belong to Christ, then you are Abraham's seed, and heirs according to the promise. (3:26-29)

Yes, we are all "sons," both males and females, and not only that but "first born sons," for we all receive the inheritance in Christ. Paul uses "sons" in the same way that the writer of Genesis used "man" in Genesis 1:27: "So God created man in his own image, in the image of God he created him; male and female he created them."

A Note on Sources

All modernized texts in this volume, except those indicated below, were drawn from Margaret Fell's, *A Brief Collection of Remarkable Passages and Occurrences Relating to the Birth, Education, Life, Conversion, Travels, Services, and Deep Sufferings of That Ancient, Eminent, and Faithful Servant of the Lord, Margaret Fell, But by Her Second Marriage, Margaret Fox...* (London, 1710). The text of *Some Ranters' Principles Answered* is drawn from copies of the pamphlet secured for the author by the late Lewis Benson of Moorestown, New Jersey, and Joseph Pickvance in Birmingham, England. Margaret Fell's first letter to George Fox, "The Mystery Letter" is drawn from the text of the original in the vault of The Quaker Collection of Haverford College, Haverford, Pennsylvania. "The Testimony of Margaret Fox Concerning Her Late Husband George Fox..." is drawn from *A Journal or Historical Account of the Life, Travels, Sufferings, Christian Experiences, and Labour of Love in the Work of the Ministry, of that Ancient, Eminent, and Faithful Servant of Jesus Christ, George Fox, Who Departed This Life in Great Peace with the Lord, the 13th of the 11th Month, 1690* (London: Thomas Northcott in George Yard, in Lombard-Street, 1694).

All scriptural citations are of the Revised Standard Version (RSV) of the Bible, unless otherwise noted. King James Version (KJV) citations are used in a few instances where that translation is intimately related to Margaret Fell's interpretation of scripture, and the modern version is so different it obscures the scriptural foundation of her argument.

Endnotes

Preface to the First Edition

1. The difference between the two groups is that the former was university trained and, in their apologist stance, massaged the Quaker message into the theological and philosophical milieu of their time. Howgill, Crisp, and Fell, on the other hand, were dynamic and powerful preachers with an apostolic vision of Christianity—prophetic Christianity. Benson explores Fox's understanding of prophetic Christianity in "George Fox's Teaching about Christ," *Quaker Religious Thought* 16 (Winter 1974-75): 20-42. Douglas Gwyn explores the vision further in his *Apocalypse of the Word: The Life and Message of George Fox* (Richmond, IN: Friends United Press, 1986).

2. *A Brief Collection of Remarkable Passages and Occurrences Relating to the Birth, Education, Life, Conversion, Travels, Services, and Deep Sufferings of that Ancient, Eminent, and Faithful Servant of the Lord, Margaret Fell...* London, 1710. In spite of its nearly 600 pages of material, it is by no means comprehensive, containing only a bare selection of Fell's many epistles, and a representative collection of her more important pamphlets. In all, Margaret Fell wrote sixteen books, four of which were translated into Dutch, two into Hebrew, and one into Latin.

3. Maria Webb's popular, *The Fells of Swarthmoor Hall and Their Friends...* (Philadelphia: Henry Longstreth, 1896) went through a number of printings. Helen Crosfield's, *Margaret Fox of Swarthmoor Hall* (London: Headley Brothers, 1913) was the second.

4. Ross's work was reissued in 1984 under the imprint of The Ebor Press, York, England, and contains certain corrections and emendations in keeping with the author's request.

5. See, for instance, Hill's *Puritanism and Revolution* (NY: Schocken, 1958); *The Century of Revolution* (NY: Norton, 1961); *Antichrist in Seventeenth Century England* (London: Oxford University Press, 1971); *The World Turned Upside Down* (NY: Viking, 1972).

6. These are the expected: traditional references to the Divinity (Almighty, Father) and divine manifestations (Son, Holy Spirit).

Chapter 1

A True Testimony from the People of God

Historical Introduction

1. For further background on this effort, see the introductions and documents in Chapter 5: Margaret Fell Fox in Her Own Words.

Epistle to the Reader

1. Readers should not be daunted by the gargantuan opening sentence: Fell's syntax will settle into easier reading.

2. The valley in which God will assemble all nations for judgment (see Joel 3:2).

A True Testimony, Etc.

1. Romans 1:9: "For God is my witness, whom I serve with my spirit in the gospel of his Son...."

2. What follows is actually a composite of passages from 1 Corinthians 3:16f, Jeremiah 31:33, and 1 Corinthians 6:19-20.

3. The law.
4. Christ.

Chapter 2

A Declaration of Quaker Principles and Practice...

The Declaration
1. See Fell's "A Relation..." (162-164) for her autobiographical remembrance of her meetings with Charles II and his court.
2. The reference is to the early Christians.
3. Margaret Fell apparently reinforces the scripture references here substantially because of the Quaker inability to take Oaths of Allegiance, a refusal which, if misunderstood, could be viewed as tantamount to treason. Margaret Fell, herself, was to know four years of suffering, imprisonment, and legal non-entity after her conviction and sentence of praemunire for refusing to take the Oath of Allegiance to the King in 1664.
4. The "respect" Margaret Fell is referring to here is not a matter of common courtesy, but a reference to the special obeisance and obsequiousness one was to show in movement and language to those of high social class. Quaker refusal to show partiality to men and women included refusing removal of the hat and using "thee" and "thou" to refer to all people, when those pronouns were used in seventeenth century England only when referring to common people. Since Quakers refused to remove the hat in Court and addressed the Judge in the vernacular, they were often cited for contempt. Thus, Margaret Fell strives to make it clear in her declaration that the ground of Quaker action is divine will, not contempt for government and law.

5. This key point will be made again in the January 1661, *A Declaration from the Harmless and Innocent People of God, Called Quakers, Against All Plotters and Fighters in the World.* That great early statement of the Quaker Peace Testimony emphasized early Friends' belief in the power of God as sufficient to vindicate the faithful, even if they were to be driven to earth. The position is grounded firmly in God's vindication of the witness of Christ whose crucifixion and death reflected the worst that could befall.

6. George Fox and Margaret Fell had personally experienced these tactics. Even as Charles II entered England in the spring of 1660, constables invaded Swarthmoor under the pretense of searching for arms during one of Fox's visits and carried Fox off to prison on suspicion of plotting against the King, a suspicion reinforced by the fact that he could not take the Oath of Allegiance.

7. These scriptural references are carefully ordered stepping stones toward the Quaker understanding of the Gospel, Timothy opening with the advice "that supplications, prayers, intercessions, and thanksgivings be made for all men, for kings and all who are in high positions, that we may lead a quiet and peaceable life, godly and respectful in every way. This is good, and it is acceptable in the sight of God our Savior, who desires all men to be saved and to come to the knowledge of the truth."

8. Margaret Fell, while attesting to the peaceable nature of Quakers, notes their militant side in her references to spiritual warfare. See the introduction to her *Declaration...,* pages 80-81, for a fuller rendering of the Quaker concept of the Lamb's War.

Chapter 4

Some Ranters' Principles Answered

Content Introduction

1. It is interesting to note that the first Quakers were also careful to place the pamphlet in its larger context. The following title page for the pamphlet reflects the fact that original Friends bound it with a much larger work by Margaret Fell, *A Testimony of the Touchstone for All Professions...*, explaining the Everlasting Gospel at length.

An Answer to the Ranters' Principles

1. This reference is to what the two demoniacs of the Gadarenes asked Christ: "Have you come to torment us before our time?" Margaret Fell appears to be suggesting the Ranters are mad.
2. Both references are to Legion, the demoniac, and stress the convicting power of Christ.
3. An allusion to the whore of Babylon, Revelation 14.
4. Fell makes a telling point here, exposing the utter lack of logic in the Ranter position.
5. This is a key argument in the faith of early Quakers: true faith begets good works. When God commands, He gives the power to obey. The individual who hears and obeys will manifest the presence of Christ in conduct. If the practice is foul, the faith must be in error. Quakers used this argument with devastating effectiveness, not only with Ranters, but with persecutors who claimed to be Christian.
6. This sentence is so garbled that it is rendered strictly as it appears in Fell's pamphlet with no attempt at interpretation.

7. The RSV translates this passage: "I, wisdom, dwell in prudence, and I find knowledge and discretion." Notice how Fell interprets the verse *in context* and condemns the Ranter's random proof-texting to suit his argument.

8. This reference is to Jesus' announcement of the coming of the Counselor or Spirit of Truth. Jesus notes that when the Counselor comes, "He will convince the world of sin and of righteousness and of judgment."

9. Fell's scriptural allusion drips with sarcasm, as she turns a neat play on the word "number." The biblical reference itself is especially pointed, "This calls for wisdom: let him who has understanding reckon the number of the beast, for it is a human number, its number is six-hundred and sixty-six."

10. Both of these passages stress the difference between the actions and practices of the faithful versus those of the unfaithful—again stressing the Quaker belief that the direction of the Divine Shepherd in one's life must, if obeyed, produce good fruit.

11. This Ranter reference is so obviously taken and interpreted out of context that it plainly is forced. Fell echoes the larger context of the prophecy, the announcement of punishment for gross evil, and turns it back on her opponent.

12. Again, the Ranter reference is so illogically torn from context that Fell leaps upon it with relish, alluding in her comments to the real import of the passage.

13. The reference is to the parable of the unworthy tenants with its stress on their wrongdoing, their ignoring the messengers, and finally their murdering of the owner's son. The Quaker insistence that the individual is the temple of God is important to Fell's interpretation here. The Ranters, in doing all manner of evil, are defiling themselves— potential temples of God. Moreover, the church as the body of believers is prostituted by their actions.

14. Fell echoes Daniel's description of the fate of Nebuchadnezzar, suggesting the Ranters are people of like nature to him, who through his pride fell to the level of the beasts of the field.

15. This is a key argument against the Ranter position. That position essentially is a lawless one. It lacks a ground for moral behavior. Fell reviews in this passage the progress through which a person must move to attain true liberty. One must first gain a sense of the law, a knowledge of one's wrong behavior before one can receive Christ as teacher and the liberty that walking by the Spirit gives. The Ranters' rejection of scripture and of the law of God is especially critical, for the early Quakers used the scripture as a measure for present experience and interpretation, and as a presenter of the law which convicts the wrong doer and opens the heart to the need for God and the guidance of Christ.

16. This passage is particularly chilling, perhaps for shock value. However, behind it may also lay the early Quaker belief in the day of the Lord's visitation, that time when God visits a person's heart seeking repentance, a time which, if ignored, might prove to be the loss of the opportune moment for repentance. Later, when wrongdoing produces its bitter outcomes in one's life and one wishes to repent, it may be too late.

17. The Ranter pamphlet has not been identified.

18. The high point and denouement of Fell's argument: Fell focuses, with the firmness of a prosecuting attorney sure of a conviction, on a major inconsistency in the logic of the Ranter argument. The prince of lies is discovered in his inconsistencies. Her relish for victory in the argument is undisguised here.

Chapter 5

Margaret Fell Fox in Her Own Words

Historical and Content Introduction

1. Mary was six years old, Susan two, and Sarah ten.

A Relation of Margaret Fell...

1. Popular in the North of England and in Scotland, Lecturing Ministers were individuals, often itinerants, who traveled to preach and explicate scripture, usually in less than formal religious occasions and often outside the recognized church structure.

2. See Fox's *Journal* (Nickalls' Edition, 113f) for his account of his coming to Swarthmoor Hall.

3. The "Sands" of Morecambe Bay could be crossed on horseback with caution at low tide and were a shortcut to Swarthmoor.

4. George Fox's own vision of the role of magistrates is discussed by T. Canby Jones in his *George Fox's Attitude Toward War* (Richmond, IN: Friends United Press, 1972), page 54f. Fox produced a leaflet in 1669, *The Quakers Testimony Concerning Magistracy*, and further clarified his views in a 1679 pamphlet, *Caesar's Due Rendered*. It is possible that the character and understanding of Judge Fell served as a role model in Fox's mind and was influential in shaping his vision.

5. Oxford English Dictionary: preferred—"To advance or promote to a position in life; esp. to settle in marriage."

6. As it became evident that the Cromwellian Period was coming (in 1658-59 to a close), persecutions and imprisonments increased, not only of Quakers, but of all who appeared to be a threat to the regime.

7. Margaret Fell had reasonably easy access to the King as a member of the Gentry. Furthermore, her lobbying efforts were intense and Quaker lobbying efforts were well planned, thorough, sustained, and at times formidable. They were by no means ineffective.

8. See *A Declaration and an Information of Us, The People Called Quakers, to the Present Governors, the King and Both Houses of Parliament, and All Whom It May Concern*, page 82.

9. The journey took from May to August. Margaret was accompanied by Leonard, Mary, and Sarah Fell, and Will Caton and Thomas Salthouse.

10. See Fox's *Journal* (Nickalls' edition, 456f) for his account.

11. Though imprisoned, Margaret Fell was not inactive. She wrote numerous pamphlets, one of which appears in the present collection: *Women's Speaking*. Copious correspondence and visitations kept her well informed. Though the four years of imprisonment is said to have weakened her health, it did not prevent her from living over thirty years more to the age of eighty-eight.

12. See Fox's *Journal* (Nickalls' ed., 554-55, 557), for his account of their marriage.

13. See Fox's *Journal*, page 557f, for his account of his efforts to free her.

14. See page 670f.

15. See Henry J. Cadbury's essay, "George Fox's Later Years," in the Nickalls' edition of Fox's *Journal*, page 719f.

16. The Persecutions of 1683-85, during which approximately 1,460 Quakers were jailed. See Cadbury's essay above, p. 734f.

17. A Protection was normally a royal grant of immunity from arrest or lawsuit to one engaged in the Crown's service. This is why the King appears surprised at the request. Obviously,

the request had its intended effect—it gained the case marked attention by King and Council. However, they could not grant her a Protection, because she was not a public official.

18. September, 1683—Rachel and Daniel Abraham had been married in March. The official contradiction between fine and imprisonment would have been comical, if significant suffering had not been involved.

The Testimony of Margaret Fell...

1. This modernized version is drawn complete from *A Journal or Historical Account of the Life, Travels, Sufferings, Christian Experiences, and Labour of Love in the Work of the Ministry, of that Ancient, Eminent, and Faithful Servant of Jesus Christ, George Fox, Who Departed This Life in Great Peace with the Lord, the 13th of the 11th Month, 1690* [Jan. 1691]. London: Thomas Northcott in George Yard, in Lombard-Street, 1694.

2. Margaret has these two imprisonments reversed. Fox was first imprisoned in Nottingham in 1649, then Derby in 1650.

3. The New Style Calendar puts this in February, 1655. The Launceston Imprisonment in 1656 was Fox's fourth.

4. See *A Declaration and an Information from Us, The People Called Quakers, to the Present Governors, the King and Both Houses of Parliament, and All Whom It May Concern,* page 82.

Appendices

George Whitehead's Testimony...

1. In 1709, Whitehead (1636-1723) was one of the few remaining first generation Quakers who could testify from long and large experience to Margaret Fell Fox's faith and life. Well educated, he served Friends as a great preacher, astute writer, and notable representative before King and Court. Like Fell, he suffered imprisonments and persecution. He became, after George Fox's death, the foremost Friend in London. His fifty plus years acquaintance with Fell brought him in touch with all aspects of her life: her faith, her ministry, her administration of support to Friends' ministers and of aid to suffering Friends, her spiritual counsel, her family life, her own sufferings for her faith, and her representation of Friends before King and Court. The title of the present book is drawn from Whitehead's sensitive description of her.

2. Whitehead may be turning a serious pun with the use of the word "Friendly" for, while Judge Fell never cast his lot with the Quakers, he was so tender, compassionate, understanding, and helpful they considered him to be one of the blessed.

3. Examples of her extraordinary plain spokenness in addressing the King may be seen in her *A Declaration and an Information from Us, The People Called Quakers...* included in this volume.

4. Whitehead's admiration for Margaret Fell's care and concern for her family was well founded in the strength of the daughters she raised. Becoming though Quaker ministers in their own right, they and their husbands proved a significant strength to both her and the Quaker movement. Only her son by Judge Fell turned out to be both a social and religious disappointment.

Bibliography

Barbour, Hugh and Arthur O. Roberts. *Early Quaker Writings: 1650-1700*. Grand Rapids, MI: William B. Eerdmans, 1973.

---. *Margaret Fell Speaking*. Pendle Hill Pamphlet #206. Wallingford, PA: Pendle Hill Publications, 1976.

Benson, Lewis. *Catholic Quakerism*. Philadelphia, PA: Philadelphia Yearly Meeting, 1966.

---. "George Fox's Teaching About Christ." *Quaker Religious Thought* 16 (Winter 1974-75): 20-45.

--- . *The Quaker Vision*. Gloucester: New Foundation, 1979.

---. "'That of God in Every Man'—What Did George Fox Mean by It?" *Quaker Religious Thought* 12 (Spring 1970): 2-25.

---. *The Truth Is Christ*. Gloucester: New Foundation, 1981.

---. Unpublished Letter to Bonnelyn Young Kunze. 30 April 1984.

---. *What Did George Fox Teach About Christ?* Gloucester: New Foundation, 1976.

Coale, Josiah. *The Books and Divers Epistles of the Faithful Servant of the Lord Josiah Coale, Collected and Published, as It Was Desired by Him the Day of His Departure Out of This Life*. 1671.

Crosfield, Helen G. *Margaret Fox of Swarthmoor Hall*. London: Headley, 1913.

Curtis, John H. "Books Concerned with Christ as Prophet." *Quaker Religious Thought* 16 (Winter 1974-75): 46-47.

Fell, Margaret. *Some Ranters' Principles Answered*. London: Thomas Simmons, 1656.

Fox, George. *The Journal of George Fox*. Edited by John L. Nickalls. London: Religious Society of Friends, 1975.

---. *A Journal or Historical Account of the Life, Travels, Sufferings, Christian Experiences, and Labour of Love in the Work of the Ministry, of That Ancient, Eminent, and Faithful Servant of Jesus Christ, George Fox, Who Departed This Life in Great Peace with the Lord, the 13th of the 11th Month, 1690* [Jan. 1691]. London: Thomas Northcott in George Yard, in Lombard Street, 1694.

---. *The Works of George Fox*. 8 Vols. Philadelphia: Gould, 1831.

Gwyn, Douglas. *Apocalypse of the Word: The Life and Message of George Fox*. Richmond, IN: Friends United Press, 1986.

Hull, William I. *The Rise of Quakerism in Amsterdam, 1655-56*. 1938.

Jones, T. Canby. *George Fox's Attitude Toward War*. Richmond, IN: Friends United Press, 1972.

Jones, W. Paul. *The Province Beyond the River: The Diary of a Protestant at a Trappist Monastery*. Nashville, TN: The Upper Room, 1981.

Kunze, Bonnelyn Young. "Margaret Fell versus Thomas Rawlinson." *Quaker History* 77 (Spring 1988): 52-54.

McCandless, John H. *The Quaker Understanding of Christ*. Philadelphia: Philadelphia Yearly Meeting, 1975.

Pickvance, T. Joseph. *George Fox on the Light of Christ Within*. Gloucester: New Foundation, 1978.

Popkin, Richard H. "Spinoza's Relations with the Quakers of Amsterdam." *Quaker History* 73 (Spring 1984): 14-25.

Popkin, Richard H. and Michael A. Singer, editors. *Spinoza's Earliest Publication? A Loving Salutation by Margaret Fell. Philosophiae Spinozae Perennis.* No. 7. Assen/Maastricht, The Netherlands: Van Gorcum, 1987.

Ross, Isabel. *Margaret Fell: Mother of Quakerism.* NY: Longmans, Green, & Co., 1949. Reissued in 1984 by William Sessions Book Trust, The Ebor Press, in York, England.

Turner, W. Arthur. *Pathways to the Light Within: A Gathering of Early Quaker Poems.* Richmond, IN: Friends United Press, 1979.

Wallace, T.H.S. "This is a Silly Poor Gospel: Margaret Fell and Pharisaism." *New Foundation Papers* #4 (April 1981): 1, 6-8.

Webb, Maria. *The Fells of Swarthmoor Hall and Their Friends; With an Account of Their Ancestor, Anne Askew, the Martyr.* Philadelphia: Henry Longstreth, 1896.

Index

Abraham, Daniel 171

Adam (first) 57, 96, 100, 108

Adam (second) 57, 96

America 128, 154, 168, 184

Antichrist(s) 25-26, 41-42

Antinomianism 122, 125, 128

Apostasy 23, 25-26, 28-29, 36, 41-47, 109-110, 178

Apostles 22, 26, 28, 35, 40-41, 43-47, 59, 61, 67, 70, 78, 85, 87,
 104, 109, 123, 125-126, 128, 130, 163, 176, 178

Askew, John 160

Askew, Mary 158, 176

Babylon 23, 36, 109

Beast 23, 36, 41-43, 56, 100, 109-110, 132, 134, 137-139,
 142-144

Bristol 126-127, 165, 167-168, 181, 183-184

Charles II 76, 79, 94, 162, 209

Christ: blood of, 71; coming to reign, 33, 48, 70; cornerstone, 32,
 61, 70, 129-130; cross of, 62-63; doctrine of, 40, 163; end of
 the Law, 37, 113; foundation, 31, 59, 61, 69-70, 79; fountain of
 all life, 30, 55, 150, 152, 157-158; gospel of, 23; judge, 36; light
 of, 24, 29, 38, 48-49, 58, 62-63; power of God, 23, 26, 31, 33,
 56, 62-63, 67, 80-81, 128, 132; reconciliation of all things, 133;
 substance, 61

Church of Christ 101

Clergy 76, 79, 99, 123

Commonwealth 71, 75, 121, 123, 126-127

Conscience(s) 25, 33, 36-39, 50, 54, 63, 66, 70-71, 83-88, 90, 146,
 161, 164, 166, 182, 187, 209

Covenant 32, 35-37, 49-50, 63-64, 71, 86, 125, 131, 143

Cromwell, Oliver 75, 180-181

Cromwell, Richard 76

Cumberland 165, 180-181

Dalton 151, 160, 177, 179

Darkness 23, 28, 36-37, 39-41, 43, 45, 48-50, 52, 54-55, 58-59, 65-69, 109-110, 112, 116, 122-123, 125, 131-140, 147, 158, 161

Day of the Lord 24, 36

Doctrine 22, 25, 28-30, 35, 40-41, 47, 50, 53-55, 66-67, 83-84, 87-88, 122, 126, 128, 163, 176, 210

England 75-76, 97-98, 121, 123, 155-156, 162, 167-169, 178, 180, 184

Eve 96, 107-108

Evil 30, 33, 35, 37-38, 57, 64-65, 67, 71, 80, 83, 95, 100, 103, 114, 123, 132-136, 138-140, 144-145, 147, 160, 173-174, 186

Faith 21, 26, 29, 31, 34, 40-42, 51-52, 61, 64, 71, 77-78, 80, 84, 86, 91, 102, 123, 128, 136, 146, 155-156, 166

Fall, The 57-58, 95-96

False Church 118-119

Farnsworth, Richard 151, 161, 175, 177-178

Fell, Judge Thomas 151, 153, 155, 161, 169, 181, 209

Fell, Margaret: convincement of, 149-152; death, 155-156, 187-188, 210; espoused women's spiritual equality, 93-120; knowledge of scripture, 93; lobbying efforts, 22, 154; Mother of Quakerism, 127, 150, 153; sufferings, 75-76, 84, 89-90, 98, 154, 160, 169-170; understanding of Book of Revelation, 23

Fifth Monarchy Men 77, 163, 182

Fox, George 21, 23, 30, 75-76, 91, 94, 98, 121, 123, 127, 149, 153-154, 156, 161, 175, 177-178

Fruits 22, 33, 42, 64-66, 88, 128

Gospel 21-25, 28, 31-32, 41, 50, 54, 56, 59, 62, 67, 69, 71-72, 77-78, 80, 85-86, 94, 96, 98, 102-103, 107, 109, 114, 118, 127-128, 154, 156-157, 174-175

Grace 67, 73, 100, 104-105

Great Whore, The 118-119

Gwyn, Douglas 23-24

Holy Ghost/Holy Spirit 40, 44, 51, 53, 62, 71-72, 112, 115, 122-123

Hope 22, 47, 51, 61, 72, 76, 91, 157

Howgill, Francis 127, 179-180

Hubberthorne, Richard 91, 179

Infallible 45, 87

Ireland 162, 167, 180, 183

Jones, W. Paul 27

Judgment 24, 36, 57, 68, 72, 87, 119, 138, 142, 151, 177

Kingdom: of God, 38, 55-58, 94, 133, 174, 210; of men, 57, 70

Lamb, The 24, 31, 56, 110, 120, 134, 139

Lamb's War 24, 80, 156

Lampitt, William 150

Lancashire 160, 167, 183, 209

Lancaster 76, 94, 160, 165-167, 171, 179-183

Law 24-25, 32-33, 36-37, 50, 60, 64, 70-71, 83-85, 88, 96-97, 101, 107, 113-114, 117-119, 122, 125, 143

Liberty 32, 44, 58, 60, 63, 72, 85-86, 88, 90, 111, 125, 128, 135, 143-144, 146-147, 163-168, 175, 182-185

Light 24-25, 29-31, 36-38, 40-41, 48-50, 52-56, 58, 62-63, 65-66, 68-70, 72, 80, 86-87, 110-111, 122-123, 125, 131-137, 139-140, 147, 161, 176

London 76-77, 94, 130, 153-155, 161-165, 167-169, 172, 181, 183-186

Lower, Thomas 168

Marsh-Grange 160

Ministers 30, 33, 37, 55, 57-60, 65-67, 93-94, 99, 112, 124, 127, 151, 156, 161, 175, 179-180, 209

Moral Relativism 122

Nayler, James 126, 151, 177-178, 180

New Creature/New Man/New Person 32, 63, 72, 126, 128, 133

Nietzsche 128

North, The 153, 167-168, 170, 180-181, 185

Oath Taking, Refusal of 77, 79, 85, 94, 164, 166, 182-184

Obedience 23, 30, 46, 58, 61-62, 71, 83, 89, 122; dis- 58, 100, 131

People of God, The 32, 82, 117

Perfect/Perfected/Perfection 57, 66, 71, 83, 100, 111

Persecution 22, 31, 64, 75, 78-79, 86, 88, 127, 154, 162, 164, 168, 174, 209

Prophecy 30, 43, 53, 113, 119

Prophesy 46, 107, 111, 113-114, 118-119

Prophet(s) 22-23, 26, 30, 35, 40-44, 54, 61, 64, 69-70, 73, 81, 83-84, 87, 101, 106, 119, 123, 125, 129-130, 137, 145, 176

Prophetic Christianity 81, 122, 125

Puritan Revolution, Collapse of 22

Quaker Peace Testimony 78

Ranters/Ranterism 121-148

Redemption 57, 95-96, 105, 111, 128

Restoration of Monarchy 22, 75-76

Revelation, John's 23-25, 30-31, 118-119

Righteous(ness) 37, 48, 51, 58, 60-61, 63-64, 70, 73, 86-87, 110, 113, 117, 122, 125, 132, 135, 138, 142-143, 146, 209

Roman Catholicism 79

Salvation 31, 33, 37, 45, 49, 57, 61, 63, 67, 83-84, 86, 89, 116, 210

Sanctified 41, 59, 61, 71, 133

Scotland 162, 170, 180-181

Second Coming, The 24, 31

Serpent 95, 100-102, 138, 146-147

Sin 31, 33, 38, 42, 55, 57-58, 66, 71, 84, 88, 103, 105, 123, 133, 135-138, 141, 143-144, 146-147

Swarthmoor 76-77, 94, 98, 150-151, 153, 160, 162, 165, 168, 173, 175, 177, 179, 181-182, 185
Temple 29, 38, 47, 51, 56, 70, 111, 116, 141, 173
That of God 32, 39, 60, 87, 125
Tithes 79, 83
Ulverston 150, 154, 175, 178-179
Unity 26, 30-32, 35, 37, 41, 47, 59, 63, 89-91, 126, 172
Westmorland 165, 175, 179-180
Whitehall 22, 182, 184
White Hall Court 170
Whitehead, George 170, 209-210
Women's Meetings 172
Women's Ministry 93-120
Worship 25, 27, 29, 31, 34, 36-38, 44, 48, 50, 67, 73, 79, 83-84, 87, 124, 132, 134, 164, 166, 173
Word, The 23, 33, 70, 131
Wrath of the Lamb, The 134, 139
York, Duke of (later King James II) 163-164, 169, 171
Yorkshire 165, 175, 180-181, 183

LaVergne, TN USA
19 August 2010
193884LV00002B/7/P